How to Dream

A motivational guide to a life of hope, success, and freedom

Deedee Cummings, M.Ed., LPCC, JD

Write your dreams here:

_____

_____

_____

_____

_____

_____

_____

_____

_____

_____

_____

_____

_____

_____

_____

_____

_____

_____

_____

_____

Published in the United States by Make A Way Media, LLC

ISBN: 978-1-951218-50-8 (Paperback)
ISBN: 978-1-951218-51-5 (Hardcover)
ISBN: 978-1-951218-52-2 (ebook)
ISBN: 978-1-951218-53-9 (audiobook)

Names and details of the author's clients mentioned in this text have been changed to protect their confidentiality. The names of some things and places are made up by the author to use for demonstration only. Every effort has been made to properly attribute quotes and summarize background stories correctly.

Front cover image by Fine Artist Charlene Mosley.

www.charlenemosley.com

Printed in Canada.

First printing edition 2024

Make A Way Media, LLC
104 Daventry Lane
Louisville, KY 40223

www.makeawaymedia.com

_____

_____

_____

_____

_____

_____

_____

_____

_____

_____

_____

_____

_____

_____

_____

_____

_____

_____

**You deserve every bit of this journey.
This is your life!**

Other books by the author

Books for kids

Love Is…
Think of it Like This!
My Trip to the Beach
My Dad's Job
Heart
I Want to be a Bennett Belle
If a Caterpillar Can Fly, Why Can't I?
Like Rainwater
This is The Earth
In The Nick of Time
Kayla: A Modern-Day Princess
Kayla: A Modern-Day Princess—Dishes, Dancing,
and Dreams
Kayla: A Modern-Day Princess—Tough as Tulle
Kayla: A Modern-Day Princess—These Shoes Were Made
for Dancing
Kayla: A Modern-Day Princess—A Little Magic
Kayla: A Modern-Day Princess Activity Book
In the Nick of Time Too

Books for adults and young adults

How to Dream
How to Dream Workbook

Contents

Why You Need This Book ix

Why I Wrote This Book xiii

One What is a Dream? 1

Two Finding Your Purpose 17

Three The Meaning of Passion 37

Four Tuning Out the Noise 53

Five Why Is It So Hard to Dream? 73

Six How to Dream 91

Seven Ways to Fuel Your Dream 117

Eight Dream Affirmations 137

Nine Put Your Dream in Motion 153

Ten Become Unstoppable 171

About the Author 186

"You have to dream before your dreams can come true."

~A. P. J. Abdul Kalam

Why You Need This Book

Dreaming is difficult. Pursuing your dreams is even harder. You have the absolute right to dream, but we've been told over and over again in a million different ways to choose the "smart" path. What's not smart about following your heart?

Society has a way of quickly funneling us along paths and into the world's workforce. My own nephew was in a youth performing arts high school, when the high school counselor—*at the performing arts school*—looked him in his face and told him a career in the arts was not smart. She asked him, "Have you thought about becoming a math teacher instead?"

Let's face it—traditional paths do not always align well with individual dreams. Add in the financial limitations that often hold us back and restrict access to all the things we need to pursue our aspirations—time, education, resources, opportunities—and it becomes even more challenging. Most of the time, it feels like we are just trying to prioritize our survival over satisfying our personal ambitions.

This thinking is so embedded in our societal structure that you may not even be aware of the daily messages you receive over the course of your lifetime—messages that tell you your personal goals are neither smart nor safe. Over time, the messages become a part of our internal dialogue designed to keep us in a box.

A box that guarantees we will show up every day as a cog in the machine.

A box that keeps us working to ensure someone else's dream will come true.

Humans, animals, and insects are all a part of nature and all are well-trained in how to ensure the survival of their leaders. Not society as a whole, but society's *leaders*. Just look at the societal model of the honeybees. The worker bees do all the necessary tasks to keep the hive running, kept in check by the queen bee's pheromones. The truth is, the vast majority of us are worker bees, trained through subliminal messaging from birth not to disrupt the delicate balance of capitalism, commercialism, productivity and efficiency. This is why you have been told that your dreams are not only silly, but a waste of time. We are trained to serve the hive, not ourselves.

Do you feel like a worker bee? Like you're buzzing from task to task, day in and day out, with no end in sight? Are your days a blur of endless hive duties? Is something out there keeping you in check? Do you ever say to yourself, "There has to be more than this?"

When will you ever have the time to breathe? When will you have the time to serve *you* and *your dreams*? This book answers these questions and will inspire you to live the life you deserve.

"Reality is wrong. Dreams are for real."
~Tupac Shakur

Why I Wrote This Book

I have spent three decades serving children and families; most recently as a therapist and author of several books about the power of hope and following your heart.

Over these years, I have met many people who have given up on their dreams, and a few who never had any dreams at all. I never get used to someone telling me they have no dreams. I am still shocked every time I hear these words from someone I meet.

While researching this book, I was surprised (though I shouldn't have been) that there was almost no information out there telling people how to dream. In fact, if you search for "how to dream" you will yield mostly results about how to get a good night's sleep. Sure, there are a million self-help books out there, but we are missing a crucial first step: How do you even begin to dream in a society that actively crushes dreams?

It is vital that you have a dream and that you take steps towards that dream every day of your life. The steps can be small, but you have to give your dream room to grow. You deserve this. It is the reason you are here.

The most depressed and despondent people I meet in therapy are those who have no vision, no dream and therefore, no hope. You need your dreams to survive. You need action towards your dream to thrive.

Dreams are hard work, there is no sugarcoating that. I'll say it again: dreams are hard work, but they are worth every ounce of energy you give them. You're already giving all that energy away … give some to your dreams.

I know what I am talking about. I am a professional dreamer. My dreams are the reason I am here. My dreams have saved my life as I have battled with my own bouts of depression. Then something beautiful happens as a direct result of my dream and I am reminded why I am here … and why I must share this message with you.

How do you
even begin
to dream in a
society that
actively crushes
dreams?

Never stop believing in the *power of you*.

Never doubt that *you have a purpose*.

Never stop hoping.

Never stop dreaming.

Never stop.

Deedee

To help you really take this information off these pages and start putting your dreams in motion, download a free journal and reflection guide at:

makeawaymindset.com/howtodreamfreeguide

One
What is a Dream?

"When my daughter was seven years old, she asked me one day what I did at work.

I told her I worked at the college—my job was to teach people how to draw.

She stared at me, incredulous, and said, 'You mean they forget?"

~Howard Ikemoto

Let's start here because I've met so many people who have no answer to this question. And yet, there are so many possible answers.

A dream is:

- freedom.
- life.
- a gift.
- your idea.
- your hope.
- your song.
- your calling.
- your legacy.
- your testimony.
- the reason you are here.
- like air to breathe.
- your passion.

- your purpose.
- fuel.
- everything.
- your ticket to the life you deserve, not the life you accept.

I am not talking about the dreams you have while you're sleeping. I mean the dreams you have while you're wide awake … the dreams that *keep* you wide awake. You know, the ones that people have repeatedly told you are a waste of time? Dreams are the whispers that keep speaking to your heart.

I am talking about vision. The thing that drives people and moves them to take action that requires risk, courage … hope. Examples of dreams are everywhere. The next time you drive down a street with stores and restaurants, look at every sign you can set your eyes on—the stores, the restaurants, the churches, the tire store, the insurance office—every one of those signs represents someone's dream. These are signs of someone's hope.

Your dream is your most cherished aspiration. Protect it, care for it, nurture it, talk to it, feed it, and love it like you would your favorite human being.

Who am I to teach you how to dream? Well, I guess you could say I am a professional dreamer. I went from highly unmotivated high schooler and college freshman dropout

Your dream
is your most
cherished
aspiration. Love
it like you would
your favorite
human being.

to college graduate, and then on to graduate student, lawyer, therapist, serial entrepreneur, author, festival founder, and now I am on to my next dream and it's the biggest dream I have ever had: Broadway producer. (More on that later.)

Despite being taught in elementary school not to, I dream all day every day. And you should too. It is the stuff that miracles are made of. I'm serious. This is not an infomercial.

This is your one magical life. What will you do with yours?

I want you to carry this book with you—whether it's a physical copy or an ebook. Put tabs on pages and highlight the reminders you need to keep you focused—because you will need reminders, multiple times a day.

At the beginning of this book, you wrote your dreams. I want you to write your *biggest* dream here:

_____

_____

_____

I know I can achieve this dream because:

_____

_____

_____

Don't be afraid to fill in these lines with your thoughts. You can achieve this dream because:

- you are breathing.
- you are strong.
- you have hope.
- dreams come true every day. Why not yours?
- you won't stop.

These are some ideas. You will have your own reason to add to these lines above.

When I come up with a title for a new book, the first thing I do is Google those words. For obvious reasons, I do not want the title of my book to conflict with another—although it can. There is more than one *Love Is*, and there is more than one *In the Nick of Time*. (Both are books I published before this one.) But what I am really looking for here, more than an existing title, is what is out there in the world about this phrase or series of words. And if this phrase is out there, how can I add to the existing conversation, while also differentiating my own experience?

I have to say I was surprised when I Googled the words "how to dream." Every single entry was about how to dream while you are sleeping. *Every single one*. How to have happy dreams or fewer nightmares, w*hile you sleep*.

These are not the kinds of dreams I spend my time talking about. I want to be wide awake for this ride. There is so much out here in this world to take advantage of. It's all just waiting for you to grab it! Life really is full of magic. You just have to find *your* thing—and we all have a thing. We were born with it. Your thing belongs to you and no one can take it from you. That alone is magical.

Whatever it is you're supposed to do is out there waiting for you. Every day I work with people just like you. I guide them, not just to find their dream, but to *grab it* and turn it into the life their heart always whispered belonged to them—even when their mind wouldn't let them believe it.

What's so special about dreams?

Many years ago, when I started my therapy practice, I learned that there were many people walking on this earth who had no dreams. This was surprising to me because I was raised by dreamers (also known as hippies), so dreaming for me was right in line with every other developmental milestone, like walking, talking, and saying your first word.

Dreaming, as it was taught to me, is an essential part of life. Non-negotiable. A *must*. If you have no dream, you have no will to live. In my family, dreaming is on par with breathing.

The ability to dream should be poured into us, in the same way that we are taught all the different subjects in school. Without a dream, you are just a rote machine.

Not even a machine, more like a rote notebook—one that that someone else filled in. And the four corners of that notebook will be all you ever are or know. That's terrifying.

I can't think of anything scarier than not exploring your own life.

It's like taking a trip to another country and never leaving the hotel. But worse because *the trip is your life*.

I could go down a rabbit hole here with why I think this is, so to avoid that, I will just say that there are structures in place that benefit from having people on the planet who *never* dare to dream.

Society attempts to categorize people into leaders and followers, implying that most of us are destined to be worker bees, while only a select few can be queens. This mindset benefits those already in power—corporations, billionaires, and governments—who want to maintain the status quo. Like queen bees releasing pheromones to keep worker bees in line, those in power use subtle influences to keep us believing we can't change our station. They tell us dreams are a waste of time and then feed us a steady diet of negativity. This serves to keep us in the regulated role of the worker bee. I'm not hating on the worker bee—I'm just saying—I was not meant to be one of them. And if you picked up this book, I don't think you were meant to be a worker bee either.

I can't think
of anything
scarier than not
exploring your
own life.

Without these limiting beliefs, what kinds of queens (or leaders) could we become? You're not confined to the role others assign you. With determination and effort, you can chart your own course and become the leader of your own life, regardless of where you started.

I am a queen bee, and queens have the luxury of dreaming, planning, directing, commanding, and receiving. And *that*, my friend, is freedom.

Beyond all that, I was born with the last name Pecchioni. It's in my blood! My dad is Italian, and I was raised hearing the story about how the Pecchionis were beekeepers in Italy. The name Pecchioni means keeper of the bee. Sometimes I talk about bees as a way to highlight how we humans live and interact in similar ways. You could say I am the keeper of the bee because of the work I do teaching other humans how to dream, grow, and thrive.

The world has convinced us en masse that dreaming is a waste of time. "Take the more practical route." Sound familiar? There is a reason we hear "stop daydreaming" *more* than we hear the encouragement to follow your heart and go for it all.

Having no dreams can not only be disheartening; it can be depressing. Anxiety, depression, and suicide are on the rise across all age groups among people of all backgrounds. A 2022 survey released by the Centers for Disease Control and Prevention found that 40% of high school students felt "persistently sad or hopeless." Twenty percent admitted having suicidal thoughts. Studies show an increase in these diagnoses for adults, too.

The COVID-19 pandemic is believed by some to have contributed to more teens feeling this way, but these numbers were rising even before 2020. It's not just lingering effects of the pandemic—it's the grind. The relatively recent addition of a flood of social media channels and cyberbullying has also contributed to an increase in teens and adults feeling hopeless. Our lives are busy, chaotic, unhealthy and loud.

If you find yourself feeling depressed, anxious, hopeless, or sad, **do not be ashamed**. There are many who struggle with these feelings. I am one of them. This is the reason I'm writing this book. I believe in the power of dreams so much that I knew I needed to share this message with you.

If you are reading these words, take this as your sign from the universe that you were destined to live a big life filled with big dreams. The big opportunities you need will fall into place. I promise you that. I am a living, walking, breathing witness and I am here, now, talking directly to you.

If you are one of the many struggling with feelings of depression and anxiety, you need to talk to someone you trust. *Today*. Someone who lifts you up, not someone who

If you are reading these words, take this as your sign from the universe that you were destined to live a big life filled with big dreams.

gives you more reasons or permission to stay down. You need to ask for help finding a therapist. Someone who will hold your hand and make sure you do this. Sometimes it takes a little time to find the right therapist, but you will.

Bring your worries into the light. You need to talk to a professional about therapy and be open to the possibility that medication may help. *Therapy works.* Keep looking for the right therapist fit and give yourself this air to breathe. You absolutely do not have to do this alone.

Dreams are a crucial part of your self-esteem and your self-efficacy.

Taking action on your dreams is a crucial part of your self-care.

Listening to the call of your heart—that whisper that tells you there is more out there for you—is the way to shut down the noise of the world. We will talk later in the book about how to block negativity and get back to focusing on the reason why you were brought to this big, strange, magical floating rock called Earth.

Next, let's talk about how you find your purpose.

What messages have I gotten over the course of my lifetime about dreams?

_____

_____

_____

_____

_____

What is holding me back from going after my dreams?

_____

_____

_____

_____

_____

Do I need to talk with a therapist? If the answer is yes, what is my plan?

_____

_____

_____

_____

_____

Two
Finding Your Purpose

"I can't imagine a person becoming a success who doesn't give this game of life everything he's got."

~ Walter Cronkite

When you find your purpose, you will feel connected to your life, this planet, and to your journey in a way that nothing will be able to replace. Dreams give us hope. Dreams guide us and remind us of why we are here. Dreams are the fuel you need to take this ride called life.

Unfortunately, dreams have kind of been beaten out of most of us. How many times did you hear "stop daydreaming" as a child? *Those daydreams meant something.* Sure, you dreamed that you had on an aluminum foil suit and you were orbiting the moon, but maybe that dream would have led to you being interested in becoming an astronaut. Instead, you were told the dream was silly, so you put it out of your mind, when what you should have been doing is breathing life into it, having fun with it, and seeing where it might take you next. We get this message all wrong. Having fun with the dream is the only way to see the potential that might exist behind the vision.

Having fun with the dream is the only way to see the potential that might exist behind the vision.

Steve Harvey was in the sixth grade when his teacher asked the class to write down what they wanted to be when they grew up. At that time, Steve had a severe stutter. Despite this, he wrote on his piece of paper that he dreamed of being on TV every week and he wanted to make people laugh. Not only did the teacher tell Steve that his dream was ridiculous, she also called Steve's mother to tell her that Steve had been a "smart aleck" in her class that day! Steve thought that he would get a spanking when he got home, but instead his father sat with him and said, "Take your paper and put it in your drawer. Every morning when you get up, read your paper. And every night before you go to bed, read your paper. That's your paper." His dad was saying: *That's your dream*. I cannot even begin to count the number of weekly shows that Steve Harvey has been on.

You—like my nephew and Steve Harvey—may have shared your dream with someone you loved or trusted, only to be told to stop dreaming and settle for the practical choice. The message is that the dream you shared with them was foolish, a waste of time, and out of your reach. So, you settled for the more concrete achievement of standing on your feet for eight hours a day and being handed $8.75 at the end of each of those hours. Minus taxes of course.

I can't let you let the world kill your dream.

Why every person must (not should, *must*) have a dream.

Every person is worthy of having hope. That means every person is worthy of having dreams. **Including *you*.**

Dreams aren't locked away in a vault for only the privileged few to access. *Dreams belong to all of us.*

Dreams float to us as messages in clouds. Everything we need to make the dream happen downloads into our hearts. We just don't know we have everything we need at the time because dreams can often feel overwhelming.

When you feel overwhelmed, quiet that noise by narrowing your focus to the next step. Don't think about all the parts or all the actions you will need to take to make the dream happen. Just do the *next* thing. The next thing is the only thing you need to worry about.

Nothing will bring you happiness like a dream. Even when that dream is a heck of a lot of work. You will go to bed at night and have trouble sleeping; you'll be so filled with excitement about what tomorrow will bring. Be good to your dream and your dream will be good to you.

Your dream will reveal beautiful, fun, and spontaneous parts of yourself you never even knew existed —parts of your mind, soul, and spirit that only a good dream can wake up. *That's purpose*.

If you feel unworthy of pursuing your dreams, then your very freedom has been taken from you. Your dreams have been hijacked!

Here's the first step: Believe you are worthy of dreaming.

If you just read that last sentence and truly don't believe that, find a therapist to talk to. This is not a funny comment or an insult. I wouldn't do that to you. Unfortunately, in our society, telling someone they need a therapist has become the same as telling someone they are nuts. This is not accurate. If you really do not believe that you are entitled to dream, I am worried about you and here is why: Believing that you are *not* worthy of a dream may mean you have no hope, or it may mean that you believe you are worthless. There is not a person on the planet that is worthless. *Not one.* We all have something to contribute.

Every human being is worthy and entitled to have a dream. Every person on the planet should have a dream.

We all have dreams as children. If you feel unworthy of pursuing your dreams, then your very freedom has been taken from you. Your dreams have been hijacked!

They were taken by time, people, and circumstances who did not see your value. But that does *not* mean you don't have any value.

Dreams are essential for the spirit and the mental health of every human being, but especially if you are a person who has ever asked the question, "Is this all there is?" That is your mind prompting you to dig deeper. That is your mind trying to nudge you to refocus and to wake up.

You have more to give. You have a purpose. Your life has meaning. You were meant to be here.

Bri

Bri started raising children at seven years old. Though her mother worked two full-time jobs, the family was always broke. Her mom was the only adult at home, and she left the house every day at 5 a.m. She did not return until very late, after most of the kids had gone to bed. By twelve, Bri was picking up kids from school. She walked to an elementary school to get her younger siblings after her classes were done at her middle school.

At twelve years old, she was responsible for getting them dressed and packing lunches. In the evenings, she took it upon herself to walk her siblings to after-school activities, such as concerts and performances that they otherwise would have missed. She did this because she wanted her siblings to have "someone in the audience rooting for them."

By thirteen, this level of responsibility became all too much for Bri and she dropped out of school in the ninth grade. No one seemed to notice and there was never any consequence to Bri's mother for this decision made by a thirteen-year-old.

By fifteen, Bri was pregnant and would now be responsible for the care of her own child, in addition to her siblings.

The entire family never progressed.

If you are working two jobs, you are hopefully working two jobs to get out of a hole, and then to get ahead. But somehow, this was never the case for Bri's family. They were routinely starting over. Bri told me that she could not remember the number of times they were evicted from apartments; it had happened so frequently that the experiences blurred together. Every time they got a little something nice (a flat-screen TV or new living room furniture) they would lose it during an eviction. For most of Bri's childhood she did not have a bed to sleep in. She and her siblings slept together on the floor under blankets, using clothes for pillows.

What messages do you think Bri got throughout her childhood about dreams?

More specifically, what messages do you think Bri got throughout her childhood about *her* dreams?

I met Bri after her son started getting in trouble at school for what was labeled by staff as hyperactive and defiant behavior. The school referred her to me to get counseling for her son. But I could not move past Bri and her story.

After a literal lifetime of raising children, Bri was tired, depressed, and hopeless. This depression carried over to her parenting and accounted for much of the behavioral difficulty that her son had in school. She was too tired to take care of herself, let alone another generation of children.

It took a while to get here, but Bri was depressed, in part, because she found herself obsessing over these words:

Is this all there is?

Bri had no identity, no aspirations, and no life of her own. She was essentially a host for other human beings, and had been trained to be that since she stepped into the world. Bri lacked purpose.

…

Though Bri's story is gut-wrenching, I have met many people in less dire circumstances who have the same thought about their life: *There has to be more than this.*

We were not made to be on the hamster wheel that so many of us are currently on: rush to get up, rush to get kids ready, fight traffic, rush to get to school or work, fight traffic, rush to get home, rush to get or make food, rush to complete homework or more work from our job, rush to get to bed, rush to get up, and … it starts all over again.

Whew! I need to take a breath. Just reading these words feels overwhelming. Yet, this is how so many of us go about our days. It is a cycle with no end in sight. Unless you break it!

Your life has meaning. Your life has purpose. And it is not to run, run, run.

If you find yourself saying "I don't have time for this book," or "I don't have the time to think about my purpose or a dream," **then you need this book more than anyone else.**

It is time to pour into you.

Give yourself just ten minutes to think about these statements below and fill in the blanks.

I believe my life has purpose because:

_____

_____

_____

I believe my life has meaning because:

_____

_____

_____

I believe my dreams are valid because:

_____

_____

_____

Now, also write these answers on an index card and carry it with you wherever you go. Your dreams are valid and necessary. *You are valid and necessary.*

If you are unable to fill in these statements with your own thoughts:

- **Schedule an appointment with a therapist.** Therapy is not just for the rich or the few. We all can benefit from talking to a good therapist in the same way we all benefit from having a good doctor, a good teacher, or a good pastor. *Add therapists to the list of people you have in your circle to care for you.* If you don't have insurance or are struggling to get by, many therapists accept Medicaid. Ask around. Call the number on the back of your medical card. Ask a friend. Ask a school. But keep asking until you find one. *Do it for you.* You will be so glad you did.

- **Talk with someone you trust deeply.** Someone who speaks life over you. Not a negative relative or friend. And not someone who makes it all about them. Talk to someone who can *hear* you. It's not even about getting feedback, it's about releasing the words into the universe. This is freeing. You move the words from the prison of your mind to the air. Make the thoughts real and say them out loud.

- **Join an in-person or online group of people with similar goals.** Give yourself one hour to hear how other people do it. Where do they find the strength? How did they access their power? What gave them the ability to block out their haters and all the negativity that life can pour on you?

- **Promise yourself a better life.** Promise yourself you will take one step a day—finish one chapter of this book, or go to one meeting, or write one notecard you carry with you and look at every day to remind you that you *deserve* something beyond what your current life looks like.

- **Do something completely different and open up.** Make a new friend who has warm, positive energy. Find an accountability partner who you trust with your journey towards coming out of your shell. Work with a consultant who can keep you focused and point you in the direction you need to go. Then make a pact to touch base and give an update to that person once a week or once a month. Keep a journal and record it all so you don't keep tilling the same ground which can be mentally exhausting.

Add therapists
to the list of
people you have
in your circle to
care for you.

Your purpose should serve you first. Then it can be a blessing to others. But you must be at the center. It is through your heart that the dream will run, grow, and thrive. If you put the purpose on someone else, the dream falls when they fall. Place it with you where it belongs, and it will be safe and protected.

Back to Bri for a moment while we wrap up talking about how important finding your purpose is. Bri started to take steps towards getting her GED. It was becoming impossible to even get hired at a fast food restaurant without a high school diploma or a GED. As she talked about this new goal, I saw an excitement in Bri I had never seen. She was able to see opportunities and the possibility of a completely different life. *A life that served her.*

Then something got in her spirit, most likely a belief that she would never be able to pass the exam to earn a GED. She heard her mother's voice in her head telling her she was safer at home—something her mother needed her to believe as a child so she would stay put and take care of her siblings. Bri ran into a couple of roadblocks and was not able to view the speed bumps for what they were: things she had to move past, not dead ends that closed off the route forever. The last time I saw Bri she told me she would not be getting her GED because she was pouring everything she had into her children. Her purpose was in them, not within.

I still think of her often and hope that she did finally complete that GED. The best way to pour into your children is by them seeing you pour into you. Pouring into you *can* be your purpose. There's nothing wrong with that. Making self-care your purpose is not only acceptable but essential. The notion that self-care is selfish is a myth we've been misled to believe. *Self-care is not selfish.* If you want your children to have more, it's up to you to show them how to get more. *You* show them it is possible. This is the greatest lesson of all: the power of modeling. Personally, I believe that I have a kickass daughter because she had a kickass mama.

Get your education first and show your children how it is done. Show your children that it is important. Show your children it is real and it *can* be done.

I will say it again because I need you to absorb these words:

Your purpose should serve you first. Then it can be a blessing to others. But you must be at the center.

When you move toward your purpose, you will find your passion.

Three promises I am making myself today:

_____

_____

_____

I believe that I have a kickass daughter because she had a kickass mama.

Three
The Meaning of Passion

"Once in a while it really hits people that they don't have to experience the world in the way they have been told."

~Alan Keightley

In American culture, we often associate the word passion with a romantic relationship. Passion is so much more than hot love—but passion is definitely hot.

If purpose is the vehicle, passion is the fuel. Passion is fervent, ardent—"barely controllable," the dictionary says. Passion is a fire.

Find your passion and you will never wonder what the answer to "is this all there is?" again. Passion is excitement for life. It is the reason why you are here. Passion gets you out of bed in the morning with a hop and a skip.

Sometimes you will hear people who are very driven describe their dream as hot like a fire. Their dreams burn inside of them, making it hard to go to bed at night, and waking them up early in the morning. They go to work at a job for someone else and it still doesn't cool down. Their purpose is so clear, and their passion is so bright, they have to carry a notebook with them to jot down all the ideas that are bubbling up inside them throughout the day. Things to do, places to go, people to contact, ideas for what comes next.

So, how do you find it? How do you find your passion?

Tracy

Tracy had a fine life. She and her husband were homeowners. They had two kids, two cars, a dog, and a fence (albeit it was not a white picket fence, but a fence nonetheless). This is what we have been told is the American dream.

Once a year, they went on a nice vacation—usually to the beach or to Disney World. A lot of people would kill for this type of annual trip. They always paid for the vacation on a credit card and spent the entire rest of the year paying for the vacation until summer came around and they did it all over again.

True, Tracy had the life that many others dream of. But Tracy also found herself wondering internally, "Somehow, someway, there has to be more for me." Especially, every time she paid the monthly credit card bill for the summer vacation that had come and gone several months before.

Whenever Tracy had this thought, she heard the voices of many people in her head telling her to quiet that voice. After all, hadn't she achieved the very life that most of us

Somehow, someway, there has to be more for me.

hope exists? Hadn't she beat the game? Hadn't she leveled up to the American dream?

Tracy felt *ungrateful.* These words rang in her head: "you are so ungrateful." Where does that come from? What is the root?

Is it ungrateful to want more? To want better?

Is there a rule about how much we can do, be, or see?

Is it ungrateful to want to pay off a vacation *before* you take it?

Is it ungrateful to dream of more than one week a year away?

Or how about one week away with the kids and one week away without the kids? Is that ungrateful? Even greedy?

Is it ungrateful to not have to worry about some major life expense looming over your head that might make this the year you do not get to vacation at all?

Is it ungrateful to not want your college plan for your two kids to be "I hope they get a scholarship?"

Is it ungrateful to lie in bed at night, stare at the ceiling, and wonder, "Is this what the next 40 years looks like?"

Is it ungrateful to dream? Or to answer the call of your heart?

No, it is not. It is *not* ungrateful to want more, but this message is delivered to us in a thousand ways to keep us in worker bee status. Tracy has the life we've all been told is the golden ring. No wonder she felt ungrateful. Meanwhile, the rich get richer, and we are still paying off that credit card debt.

I encouraged Tracy to come out of her shell and join a local incubator for women entrepreneurs. Tracy had heard of the incubator group, but did not feel she was qualified to join. She had not found her passion yet and had no idea what she could do to start her own business. I encouraged her to attend one meeting, and when Tracy returned to me after that one meeting, she was on fire. Her mind was exploding with ideas. She said she had to keep the notes app open on her phone at all times to record all the thoughts she was having—she was afraid to let any of them slip away—even in the middle of the night.

Most of all, Tracy was excited about life. Though her life was nowhere near as hectic as Bri's, it was still a life on a hamster wheel with no end in sight. She did the same things every single day and found little meaning in her work or in the contributions she made to society.

More than anything else, Tracy wanted to set an example for her children. She wanted to show them that life is magical, and anything is possible. Tracy wanted to show her children that life can be anything you make it. If you can think it, you can do it. Tracy strongly desired that her children would go for it all. So, what did that mean? Tracy had to go for it all.

She decided that she would use the skills she had learned on her job—skills she enjoyed doing very much. Tracy loved building websites. She worked during the day and made a short-term sacrifice to start building websites for entrepreneurs (some of whom she met in the incubator group) at night.

And a sacrifice it was. Tracy felt tremendous guilt when she had to miss some of the kids' games or when she was occasionally late picking them up from practice. There were many occasions she questioned the time she had to put in—time away from her family. But she reminded herself that this would not last forever. Short-term sacrifice; long-term gain.

Tracy found her purpose (putting her entrepreneur dreams first, which would secure her family's financial security for generations to come) and she had found her passion (helping other female entrepreneurs communicate their dreams through websites and branding).

Five years later, Tracy owns her own company, sets her own schedule, never misses a game, and has other employees holding down the business when she is not available. Most importantly, she vacations *when* and *where* she wants to, with the kids, and without the kids *completely debt-free*.

It's real. I have seen it over and over and over again, including the testimony of my own journey. Yet, we never think these dreams can happen for us.

They can. And with your newly discovered passion, *they will.*

Here are my top tips for finding your passion in life

Embrace the journey that is your life.

Break the cycle of thinking of life as something that happens *to you* and make it something you actively create. Every day.

Know that everyone's path is different. You might come to me and say, "Well, I went to that incubator you talked about and it sucked." What works for one may not work for the next. Be open to looking for inspiration. It takes time, but *it will come when you trust that it will.*

Pour into you.

Here's where many people tell me they don't have time … *but you do.* I'm looking square at you. Your dream cannot be Plan B. *Your dream must be Plan A.* If your dream is always on the back burner, how will you ever get to it? Wake up twenty minutes earlier. Grab your favorite coffee or tea and spend time with your dream to-do list. The twenty minutes you scroll social media on your break *can* and *should* be twenty minutes you give to your dream.

What are a few small steps you can take today? What can you Google? What question can you answer? Find one person who is doing what you want to do and ask them out for coffee. Figure out what makes you the happiest in life and explore how to turn that into a career.

Be patient, but be persistent.

Hold on to this because you will need it:

Failure is a necessary part of success.

Say it again, *failure is a part of success.*

You cannot be truly successful without failing. It is impossible to learn to walk without falling. Falling is how you perfect the walk!

When it comes to dreams, people often run into failure and interpret that as a sign that their dream is silly, a waste of energy, or that all the haters were right. You stumble and immediately say to yourself, what was I thinking—I'm wasting my time. Failure is a part of the journey, and without it, you cannot build the best and strongest dream possible.

Failure makes your dream better.

Take a break. Take a walk. Reassess. Realign. Get feedback, but don't quit.

Expect fear.

Think back to anything you have done for the first time. It's always anxiety-provoking. Just go ahead and expect that. Expect that there will be times that you are afraid, and you want to quit.

Talk to your fear and say, "I knew you would show up. It's okay, I'm ready for you."

Self-doubt and a fear of failure are dream killers. If you don't plan for it, then when they show up, you are surprised, and it shakes your foundation. Sometimes it shakes your foundation so badly that you ask yourself, "Who did I think I was to begin this?"

But when you expect them, you are not caught by surprise. You knew it would come because it comes for all of us. Then you can look fear in the face and say, "Hi fear, here have a seat. Talk to me. What are you trying to tell me? What message did you bring me? What do I need to know? Oh, is that it? Okay. Thanks for telling me. I am prepared. Have a good day. Goodbye." Just to drive the point home, you can also walk over to the door, open it, and do a dramatic wave with your arm to usher the fear all the way out of your space. Then shut the door firmly behind you.

This stuff really works. Try it. It was a past President, Franklin D. Roosevelt, who said in a speech to the nation, "We have nothing to fear, but fear itself." This is true. **The *message* fear brings is never as bad as the *feeling* fear brings.**

Spend time alone.

You cannot truly assess where you have been and where you are going if you always have noise coming in. You must take time to sit in quiet, walk in nature, or meditate in the sun to truly hone in on your inner voice for guidance. This is how your dream floats to the top of your mind and finds you.

Building the best dream possible is an ongoing event. Stay curious. Stay open. Stay the course.

Take action unannounced. Announcing steps brings criticism which could drive you back into your shell. You don't need to update people on social media about what you are working on.

Being quiet is one of the hardest things to do in our society. The world is very loud and growing louder.

Next, let's talk about how a dream floats to the top of your mind.

The message fear brings is never as bad as the feeling fear brings.

Say to yourself out loud, "I want more." What is the message your brain tells you in response to this statement?

_____

_____

_____

_____

_____

What are the messages that hold you back from pursuing your dreams and where are the messages coming from?

_____

_____

_____

_____

_____

List a few small steps you can easily take today to move closer to your dream.

_____

_____

_____

_____

_____

Four
Tuning Out the Noise

"I don't focus on what I'm up against. I focus on my goals and I try to ignore the rest."

~Venus Williams

I love Venus and Serena Williams. If you pay attention to them, you'll notice a sense of calm around them. You can't tell them nothin'. And they know it!

I once saw an interview with Venus where she was asked how she deals with reporters asking her questions. Many athletes will tell you how draining and emotionally invasive press conferences can be. The kinds of questions that athletes are often, by contract, forced to sit there and listen to can be filled with little bombs of negativity and energy killers.

When a reporter asked Venus how she handles the pressure of these conferences, she coolly said, "For me, personally, how I deal with it is that I know every single person asking me a question can't play as well as I can and never will. So, no matter what you say or what you write, you'll never light a candle to me."

Damn.

Was that cocky? Hell yes it was, and I loved every word. Do you want to chase down your dreams with all the passion and purpose God gave you? Then I'm gonna need you to be a little cocky. That's how you talk to fear at the table when it comes in and sits down right next to you.

The world is loud.

The world is a very loud place and it grows louder every day. Only by becoming a little arrogant about your vision will you be able to keep all that negativity at bay.

Get cocky about your vision. Get cocky about your goals. When you become the expert on your vision no one in the world will be able to light a candle to you. There is nothing they can do or say to shine a light on you and expose anything but the goodness taking place. The more of an expert you are, the more quiet the world becomes.

Nothing clears noise like focus.

Be very mindful about how much time your phone takes from you each day. Track your daily screen time. We are now conditioned to walk around with these little computers in our hands. I have often said that one day they will just be embedded in our hands to make things even easier for us. We will never lose our phone again or have it stolen. It will live with us 24 hours a day and we will have to plug ourselves into the wall to recharge. The phone that is embedded, that is—not ourselves—if only it were that easy for us to recharge ourselves.

I saw an article recently where a man was talking about how he used to read ten or more books a month. He barely reads one book a month now, because of all the podcasts, streaming channels, games, and social media avenues he can now explore.

Look around a restaurant the next time you are out and see how many tables of people are completely checked out from one another, preferring to scroll their phones instead of communicating directly with each other. I wouldn't be surprised if they were replying to a group text or commenting on a social media post or email with one of the recipients right there at the table.

When I go for a walk at the park, toddlers are no longer content (or maybe it's the parents who are not content) with just strolling in the walker, feeling the breeze on their faces and taking in the trees, the birds, and the clouds. Now they watch an iPad on the journey instead.

Noise is everywhere.

If you continuously listen to podcasts or videos, scroll social media, play video games, talk on the phone, blast music or spend your nights replying to emails—how will you ever get to you and your dreams? You can't become the expert in your field by watching others make moves on social media. It doesn't work that way.

How will you hear your thoughts when your mind is flooded from every angle with the thoughts of others?

You have to be intentional about this very prevalent habit in our society and consciously tune out the noise in your life.

Angelo

17-year-old Angelo was referred to me by his high school counselor for therapy. He was described as "angry and defiant." He was expected not to graduate from high school with his class that year.

Angelo lived in a chaotic environment. His father and his father's live-in girlfriend had a combined five children. Angelo and his father agreed that there were arguments every single night between dad and his girlfriend. Though the arguments never turned to violence towards one another, they were filled with screaming, and sometimes resulted in things being thrown and broken. There were also a lot of slamming doors and children crying.

Angelo often spent his nights in the corner of the bedroom he shared with his brothers, under the covers, AirPods in ears, watching TikTok, YouTube or Instagram live. He often was surprised that time got away from him, and all of a sudden, it was three or four in the morning. At that point he would switch over from videos and reels to music and try to go to sleep, needing to get up by 5:30 to catch the bus by 6:00 to get to school by 7:00.

He never missed the bus—he made it to school on time every day. But he was never motivated to participate in class. Exhausted, he had fallen behind and found it difficult to jump back into new material. He was failing everything, and he was pissed off when people would ask him why. To Angelo, the reason why he was failing was obvious; anyone who had the nerve to ask had clearly not been paying attention to the mess that was his life.

But Angelo had dreams. He just had no idea where to start. Angelo had no model, no purpose, and no passion. What Angelo did have was a small voice that would whisper to him, "You are greater than this."

Angelo's mother passed away when he was nine. Before she died, she told him about how her father had owned property and been a very successful businessman who was able to provide well for his family and his community. Angelo had the same dream, but he was discouraged because he was lost in school, and he felt that he had squandered his chances to be the successful businessman his grandfather had once been.

I asked Angelo to map out his patterns for me—what his days looked like—and how much time he spent on social media. Angelo estimated that he spent approximately TEN hours a day on social media. Worse, Angelo couldn't really tell me anything he gained from social media. Social media is not a negative thing, but it should be used for entertainment and education, and even then it should be in moderation. If you can't tell someone else what you have gained, then you have wasted the one thing you cannot get back: time. I can't think of anything worth doing ten hours a day that is not geared towards building you, your future, or your bank account.

Angelo had fallen into a social media trap of sorts. Never really meaning to give it that kind of time. (Sound familiar?) He found himself in a pointless cycle of mindless, endless scrolling as he bounced from one platform to another looking for something—anything—to engage his brain.

This is an addiction.

Social media is noise, and once you become addicted, it can become very harmful to your development—no matter how young or old you are. This does not mean that social media can never be a part of your life. It means that *you* need to be in control of *it*; not *it* in control of *you*. And for far too many of us, social media sucks us in and wastes way too much of our time.

I have put my phone down before, determined to complete a project, and then suddenly been completely surprised that my phone somehow ended up in my hand. My subconscious led me to pick up the phone. To see what video is playing next. To be entertained. To be mindless. To scroll. It can absolutely be addictive. And it is even worse for teenagers who have not learned how to manage all their inhibitions yet.

At seventeen, Angelo was already sick of his life. He was so unhappy, in fact, that he decided to go cold turkey on social media, removing all the apps from his phone. He talked with a counselor at school about enrolling in a dual program to finish high school while obtaining a barber's license at a local community and technical college. And he made a plan to continue in his grandfather's footsteps.

There were times when Angelo's father and his girlfriend still argued, but they became less frequent, because they made an agreement with the kids to leave the house and argue in the car or to reserve the argument until morning when the kids had already left for school. The arguments were not eliminated, but they were far less, making it easier for Angelo to not feel the need to escape into an app on his phone.

With the help of therapy to improve his mindset, Angelo graduated from high school and got his barber's license. Just two years later, with the help of a local entrepreneur program, he bought his first building. The business was housed in an old shotgun-style house converted to a commercial building, where Angelo and three barbers who worked under him cut hair. Angelo was paying himself rent and making income from his own services, in addition to the services provided by three other professionals. He was well on his way to his second property before the age of twenty.

...

It is never too early to begin a dream.

What are you willing to tune out to make it happen? Sometimes it's social media. Sometimes it's other people. It might be your own mind that whispers how impossible your dream may be. Get clear on what you need to tune out in order to focus on the reality of your dream, because dreams come true every single day.

The world is loud. Your dreams have to be louder.

Perhaps the loudest noise of all can be the voice in your head. It can be one voice (your father's, your grandmother, an ex) or it can be many (the people in your circle).

You have to be very careful about who you let in your head. This is why social media is so dangerous for kids. As a parent, you would never let a stranger knock on your door, say "I have something to tell your kids," and then stand back and let them in your home. Yet, this is exactly what happens when kids are on social media. Strangers are delivering messages that fill their heads with things you will never even know about because you will not be able to keep up with all the videos they have been exposed to.

The world
is loud. Your
dreams have to
be louder.

And the same thing happens to you. Our minds don't have the time to process everything we see, hear, and feel, so these messages get tucked away and stored. When something happens that is related to what you've seen or heard, those messages come back and affect your thoughts and your decisions in ways you are often not aware of.

Your brain is a rich garden where all kinds of good stuff grows. Instead of tomatoes and cabbage, your brain grows ideas.

If you were a gardener, you would carefully choose your soil, you'd give it the fresh fertilizer it needs, water, sunlight, and pruning. Take care of your brain the same way.

Watch how fast your brain grows when you prune things like hours of social media and negative energy from your life.

Having a positive circle in your life is crucial. Going to law school is probably the most difficult thing I have ever done. It was long. And it was *arduous*.

I did not go to law school full-time because I still had to work full-time, so I was in for five years, not three. It is the only thing, since my daughter came into the world, that I can recall wanting to quit. But my beautiful husband, Anthony, was all in. I hadn't realized that when I applied to go to law school, he applied too. When I got admitted, he got admitted too. One night I was crying, it was late, I had heartburn (for the first time ever), I was taking Constitutional Law (for the second time) and my head was throbbing. I said, "I can't do this anymore. I am going to quit." And Anthony said these words exactly, "You can't quit. We've come too far."

You know what? He was right. I had fewer classes in front of me than I had behind me. But I needed someone to remind me of that. To pick me up, dust me off, throw me a bottle of water, an antacid, and an "I believe in you" and point me in the right direction again. Most importantly, I was reminded that I was not alone.

When I graduated, Anthony graduated too.

I know how fortunate I am to have that in my own home. Sometimes it is hard to get away from negative energy. You may be surrounded by it at work. It may be a parent. You may be married to it. But living with it does not mean you have to allow it to take root in your mind.

Here is how to handle a negative person:

A negative person who does not realize that they are a negative person:

> Know with every fiber of your being that they are not really talking to you. Sure, they are looking you in the eye and using your name, *but they are not talking to you*. About 90% of what people say *to you* has absolutely nothing to do *with you*.

You see, these are the kinds of gems you learn in therapy.

Example: You are about to head out when your grandfather comes through the door and says, "It's hell out there."

On that statement alone, you turn around, take your shoes off, and sit back down on the couch. What was he talking about? What did he mean? Do you even have any idea, or did you just allow yourself to absorb these words? Your grandfather told you about a feeling. You absorbed them as a fact.

He may have been talking about work, but you don't work at the same place. He may have been talking about traffic. But he was in a car in gridlock. You are on a bike. You are not going to have the same experience. Because he is older, maybe wiser, maybe someone you even trust, you heard that four-word statement and called it quits on the spot. That statement was about his experience—his journey—not yours.

Know that when people make statements, they are often talking about themselves, even as they tell you they are talking to and about you. Sometimes people think they are looking out for you, helping you see how things really are, cushioning the blow, keeping it real. The problem is, they are most often talking about their own life. Their words and thoughts on the matter have *nothing* to do with you.

A negative person who absolutely knows that they are a negative person:

Boundaries, boundaries, boundaries. To the max. Do not share any part of your dream with them. A negative person who knows they are negative will make it their mission to tear your dream apart. This is because they are not happy with themselves. They will get in your head because that is what they do. Because of their negativity, they can't get ahead, and they don't want anyone else to either.

Remember earlier in the book when we were talking about loving on your dreams like you would love on your favorite human being? Would you allow your children or someone else you love to share their dreams with this person and have them crushed? No? Then don't share your dreams with them, either.

Put up a boundary and hold the line. You owe them nothing. *I don't care who they are.* And remember: Just because someone says something does not make it a fact.

Feelings are not fact. Feelings are feelings and everyone has a different set of feelings about any given subject. Listen to your own feelings on the matter at hand and do not invite their feelings into your mind.

If they throw a zinger at you before you can get away unscathed, stop right where you are. Take the words that they just said to you, put the words in an imaginary trash bag, walk over to a trash bin and throw those words into the can. Leave the words there and walk away. Do not carry them with you. Do not allow them to enter your aura. Dismiss them outright. We do not have to accept and inhale the messages people deliver to us. We do not have to allow the words to become a part of our journey or who we are.

Often, people who are not happy with themselves try to project their experience with life onto you. They did not make it, so they will try to tell you that you can't make it.

Don't ever take advice from people who have no dreams.

Don't ever take advice from people who have small dreams.

Only take advice from people who have done and are doing the work. Even then, pick and choose the advice that applies to you and your situation.

Don't ever take advice from people who have small dreams.

Stay calm. Stay focused. Negativity is a *major* distraction. Blowing up and becoming angry "because you have the right to" is a distraction. Spend time learning how to *respond*, not react. Don't take negativity personally. It is rarely about you. Don't allow it to follow you into your space. Don't internalize it. Don't take it with you. Set it down. Leave it right there.

Nothing blocks noise like taking action.

Want to show them that they crossed a boundary? Take the next step toward your dream.

Some things I need to limit or remove from my life are:

_____

_____

_____

_____

_____

_____

_____

_____

_____

Five
Why Is It So Hard to Dream?

"If your world doesn't allow you to dream, move to one where you can."

~Billy Idol

D reaming is not for the faint of heart. It takes a belief in something bigger than you and something my mother, Andrea Pecchioni, used to call sticktoitiveness. Yes, that's a real word and it's a fantastic one to boot.

Write that down: sticktoitiveness. Thank you, mama.

I'm talking about tenacity.
The ability to hold on.
To take a nap and get back up.
To believe that the sun will rise every morning.
That caterpillars magically turn into butterflies.
That flowers will remember to rise again in the Spring.
That stars can guide our path.
That light always follows darkness.
I'm talking about believing in the *power of you*.
You, my dear, are the light.

You already have all the sticktoitiveness
inside you that you will ever need.

75

You just have to activate it. Put it in motion. Get it flowing.

Here's what humans have in common with bees. We live in a society that *actively* discourages people from achieving their personal goals. In a bee colony, the roles of the queen bee and the worker bees are highly structured.

Just like in the hive, our society needs us to fill certain roles, or the way society has been structured for us won't work. The forty-hour work week. Hamburgers and hot doughnuts twenty-four hours a day. Groceries straight to your door seven days a week. Planes, trains and buses that all run on time (for the most part). This is all structured, an expectation set in place by the people who make the rules. There are businesses that close on Sundays and we accept that. That means this can be done, and it will all be okay, *if the people in charge make that the rule.*

Think back to the pandemic when jobs and services were disrupted. People became very upset when their favorite restaurant closed, or there were only two cashiers checking people out at the mega grocery store, or when none of us could find toilet paper. While not all of this was attributable to a reduced workforce, a lot of it was. People were at home and had time to think, breathe, and dream. They had time to make podcasts and YouTube channels that made them income. They were writing books and holding classes on Zoom. They were catching up on sleep!

Good for them.

But for the people in the drive-through, and the people in line at the grocery store, it was sheer chaos. I heard people behind me in the line pissed off and loudly proclaiming, "Where are all the worker bees?"

Our communities were not operating smoothly—everything from filling potholes in the street, to ensuring we have a supply chain that can get us toilet paper, to operating in partnership with the rest of the world was out of balance.

What happened next? Wages went up. In order to get some of the worker bees back, you had to pay them a little more. What a novel idea. It is all part of the structure of our society. The worker bees do not make these rules.

One purpose of the hive mentality is to allow us all to live in a society together and, for the most part, operate smoothly and keep everyone content. Busy as a bee, but content. But another purpose is to serve the queen—which in this analogy could be government, corporations, shareholders, or billionaires.

Society, just like a hive, places high emphasis on efficiency and productivity, often discouraging activities that might be seen as less practical or not to the benefit of the group as a whole (like personal goals). In fact, societal leaders and institutions don't outright say this, but they regularly enact laws, policies, and initiatives that prioritize (what they believe is) the greater good. But often it is really *their* greater good, prioritized over individual aspirations. Think healthcare tied to your employment as a way to make it harder to quit your job or go out on your own and start your own business.

I always tell the entrepreneurs I work with that *you have to prioritize your own ideas about what that greater good really is.*

What does the greater good mean to you, because most likely it does not mean the same thing to the company you work for.

Taco Hut does not want you to dream because Taco Hut *needs* worker bees. When you take the time to work on your dream, your ideas about what "greater good" means will be vastly different from Taco Hut's ideas about what it means. And they will hold "benefits" like healthcare for you and for your family over your head.

The very thing that breathes life into you—your dream—will be seen as inefficient, a distraction, not practical, irresponsible, and a complete waste of time by not just those in power, but also by those who are completely okay with handing over their power to someone else.

Know who you are dealing with before you invite them into your dream.

Much like humans on the hamster wheel of life's hectic five, or even six- and seven-day work week, worker bees follow a very regimented lifestyle that is full of tasks that can never be completed. This is how the queen bee maintains order—by keeping you too busy, too frantic, to dream. You could drop dead on the job and the queen will summon another worker bee to step right over you and keep the machine running. What was that we were saying about greater good again?

During the spring of 2020 (at the start of the pandemic) we were all forced to sit still. Restaurants were closed. Offices were closed. Schools were out. The vast majority of us, with the exception of medical personnel (God bless them), were home. In early summer, the horrendous murder of George Floyd was broadcast in totality on TV. We all saw it. We were all a witness, and the masses took to the streets. Day and night. All across the world to call attention to the injustice that Black people face in America and worldwide.

Why did the world respond so massively to the murder of George Floyd? *We had the time and the energy* to protest. The beehive was closed! We had the mental bandwidth to speak up about injustice because we were not fighting traffic and rushing to work and fighting with our kids over homework in the evening. We had the time. And we had the energy.

And what did the then President say in response? "Everybody back to work!"

The hive was disrupted. All the worker bees were in the street and this, not necessarily the pandemic itself, was bad for business. Greater good.

This is an example of how a challenge to the way things have always been (the status quo) and a shift in control (protesters in the middle of the street, everywhere) will be resisted by those in power. This is an example of how the greater good will be shifted back by those in power. The world *needs* worker bees and it *needs* them to be at work.

But it happens every single day on a smaller scale too.

Keisha

Keisha was a consulting client of mine and she had lived the vast majority of her life being "miserable." She told me her entire life "never felt like her life." She wanted to be a Broadway actress, but her mother said that was the most ridiculous thing she'd ever heard of. "No one from Louisville, Kentucky becomes a Broadway actress," were her mother's exact words. (I'm looking at you Kayla Pecchioni!)

Keisha wanted to go to college at an HBCU (historically Black college or university) like Bennett College in North Carolina or Hampton University in Virginia, but her mother said that was a waste of money "and no one would hire an HBCU graduate in the real world." (Now I'm looking at me!)

Keisha's mother told her the "practical" thing to do would be to go to community college for two years and then transfer to the local university to finish her degree. This would save Keisha money and she could still stay in town to help out the family, who was caring for a grandmother with dementia.

Keisha did stay in Louisville and attended community college as her mother recommended, but she never finished her college degree. Keisha said her mother's voice, as well as the voices of other family members, dominated her thoughts: "Why give your money to a university when you could give it to yourself?"

Simply put, when Keisha's personal goals were taken out of the equation, so were her purpose and her passion—and it all added up to zero dreams being accomplished. Practicality is a dream killer.

Keisha, desperate to get away from the negativity, got an apartment and a job. Soon that became Keisha's whole life. She became stuck. She was miserable—that's the word she used. One day Keisha looked up and all of a sudden, she was fifty-five years old and depressed. After more than three decades in worker bee status, she felt she had nothing to show for it—no home that she owned, "no family of her own," no savings and no plans.

Practicality is a
dream killer.

She felt she died a long time ago, and she asked me, "Is this all there is?"

Keisha had been married once, briefly. She left her apartment and moved into her husband's house, but she said the negativity lived in her head and destroyed the relationship. She never believed she was worthy of "good things" like love, hope, or dreams. Keisha said, "I believed I was unlovable, so I acted unloveable. I do not blame him for asking for a divorce."

She worked her whole life at a job that never appreciated her, with wages that never fully adjusted to inflation, keeping her trapped with no time to dream and no path to learn how.

I encouraged Keisha *to dream*. To think about what she does well and then to network with other people in a variety of ways, because you just never know what opportunities will fall out of the sky when you put yourself out there. All the while, we worked on canceling the negative voices in her head so when opportunity finally came calling (and it would) she'd be ready.

Then she joined a Facebook group. Thanks to her father, Keisha had been a lifelong Chicago Bears fan. She started following a group that talked about all things Chicago Bears. One Sunday afternoon before a game, another local fan commented, "I wish I could find some wings—no one makes good wings anymore."

Keisha commented, "I'll make you some wings."

That simple reply led to Keisha preparing large pans of wings for all kinds of sports fans all over the city. Each order was lovingly made right in her own kitchen. Soon, she got more orders than she could handle and had to hire help to prepare the orders.

Eventually, a friend helped her make a Facebook page and a website for her wing business. Later, she expanded her menu. One of the most popular items she made were jars of homemade pickles, which Keisha greatly enjoyed. She loved making pickles and, prior to this, often made them and gave them away. When Keisha told me this, I had no idea that pickles were even that popular. She made jars and jars and jars of pickles in a wide variety of flavors: dill (which I never knew was a flavor—I just thought that's what a pickle was), jalapeno, honey mustard, sweet and sour, horseradish, Ranch, salt and vinegar, garlic, and I kid you not, Kool-Aid flavored pickles! They were a hit!

Keisha was able to get a new car, get her hair done once in a while (which made her feel great), and for the first time ever, she had real savings. The manager on the job where she had been for more than thirty years "found" her Facebook page (with the help of another worker bee) and told her that she never signed an agreement for secondary employment. The manager gave her an ultimatum: close the side business and sign the form or be fired immediately.

Though Keisha was not ready to go it alone with her business just yet, Keisha quit her job of over three decades right there on the spot.

She was worried and had no idea how she would make ends meet, but Keisha had a power she never felt before. For the first time ever, Keisha felt that she was in absolute control of her own destiny. Keisha believed in the power of Keisha.

She was amazed by how much time she had to dream, plan, work on her website, work on her recipes, and market her own business without a job to report to every day. Most of all, she was rested and off the wheel. After thirty-seven years of supporting someone else's dream, Keisha was finally pouring into hers and it paid off. Big. The business was flourishing because she had a passion for wings and pickles. Actually, her passion was deeper than that. She had a passion for feeding others and bringing them joy through food. Keisha had an ever-growing fan base thanks to the connections that began in a group of football fans.

Recently, Keisha enrolled in acting classes to fuel her soul. She took a trip to New York and saw a couple of Broadway shows for the first time in her entire life. Her passion for cooking is now fueling her lifelong passion for theater and acting. Who knows where Keisha will go next? Dreaming is all about taking the next step—and that is exactly what Keisha is doing.

When you activate one dream, your spirit becomes like a locomotive. You hitch one idea to the next and before you know it, you are a high-speed engine hooking one car to the next car to the next. Dreams make you unstoppable.

...

It is never too late to begin a dream.

What are you willing to walk away from to finally put your dream in motion? What are you willing to do differently? What new thing are you willing to try? What limb are you willing to walk out on ... even when it's scary?

The hive—in other words our community—has a set agenda that prioritizes the collective over the individual.

This means there will never be time for you to follow your own ideas about what your life should be, unless you *demand* it and decide that *you alone* are a worthy priority.

Keisha, you alone are worthy of love. And so are you, the person holding this book.

Dreams are often seen as revolutionary because you are challenging the status quo (again, meaning the way things have always been) and causing a shift in dynamics which will often be resisted by those in power. Dreams shake things up.

Dreams make you unstoppable.

I believe it irritated Keisha's manager's spirit that she seemed to be doing so well. As a result of witnessing Keisha's success, other people were buzzing about and whispering that they had ideas and dreams too. When the manager confronted Keisha and she quit, he spread the rumor that she'd been fired. In the same way the queen bee sprays her pheromones, the manager was attempting to get all the worker bees back in line and afraid to dream, afraid to break free from the suffocating routine of the hive.

We receive so many messages that hold us back, that keep us fearful and in a box. Do not be afraid. Just keep doing the work. Take the next step. You will always be a rundown worker bee if the queen has her way.

What new things are you willing to try to move closer to your dreams?

_____

_____

_____

_____

_____

_____

_____

_____

Six
How to Dream

"The biggest adventure you can take is to live the life of your dreams."

~Oprah Winfrey

START NOW.

Did that first line startle you? Good. As my grandmother TazMay, would say, let's get to going!

Did you even realize that you had already begun your dream journey by reading this book? Congratulations, you're on your way! Hold on to your dream. Don't lose sight of it when you put this book down. Promise yourself that you are on the road to freedom and the journey has begun.

Your dream is a cherished aspiration. Love it like you would a dear sister. Nurture it like a child. Date it like a partner. Talk to it like you would a trusted friend.

Once a child asked my daughter, Kayla, "How do you find your dream?" I was so proud of Kayla when she answered without missing a beat, "You don't have to worry. Your dream will find you." I thought, "I made that!" This is the perfect answer and it is so very true. Reach out for your dream and it will also be reaching out to you.

Your dream has a life of its own. The life that you want. It's okay to talk to your dream. People might call you crazy, but they can call you crazy all the way to the bank.

Ask your dream, "What do you need from me today? Have I made you any promises I did not keep? Who do I need to call? What information do I need to look up? Are you waiting on anything from me?"

Then wait for your dream to answer.

I love the cover of this book. It was designed by my very good friend and fine artist Charlene Mosley. Charlene is the illustrator for many of my children's books. We dream together all the time and we are both inspired by nature. Charlene goes to the mountains. I go to the beach.

Come out from behind four walls and look to the skies.
There are answers there, waiting on you.
Dreams can't reach you in a cubicle.

Dreams reveal your true potential. The more you give it, the more you will get. Following your dreams is like signing up to take a college course all about you—you will learn so much about yourself. And you'll never regret a day spent on your dream.

Dreams reveal your true potential.

Be clear on what your dream is … and what it is not. Make that date I mentioned with your dream. ***Put it on the calendar.*** Spend time with just you and your dream. Talk to it and listen to it. Treat it like you would any valued relationship. Don't neglect it. Don't set it on the back burner. And don't let anyone else who has not had a track record of achieving dreams tell you what to do with it.

If you feel like you have no time for yourself, that is precisely the reason you must make the time. Life will continue to absorb everything you have. Intentionally plan to give something to yourself.

Introduce your dream *only* to those who truly deserve to meet your dream. **Learning about your dream is a privilege.** Hearing the story behind what makes your heart float and gives your mind hope is *special*. Everyone does not deserve an invitation to the party.

People will usually not flat-out state that your dream is a waste of time. If they did, it would save us both a whole lot of trouble. No, most of the time people drop what I call little dream-killing bombs along the way. They will couch it in terms like, "I'm not trying to be negative. I'm just trying to be real." They are *not* helping you. They are *not* doing you a favor. They are talking to their *own* fears. And you don't need that. You need people who have an uncommon kind of faith.

Move with intention and be in control of every move you make. Don't ever hand important parts of your dream over to someone else. You are in control of the decisions and the direction. Last summer, I read the play *A Raisin in the Sun* by Lorraine Hansberry. I had also previously seen the movie, but reading the words for some reason spoke louder. In the play, the adult son is a huge dreamer. The problem? He had no real passion for his dream, because he wanted something that came too fast and too easy. Worse, he put his money in the hands of someone else and (spoiler alert) that person ran off with every dime he had. He was left with nothing because there were no real roots to the plan, and he was not in control of the next step when it came to his own aspirations.

Cherish your dream. Know that it is real and will be made even more real with the work you put into it. If you feel like you are merely surviving, you are in doggy paddle mode. Do you know how to doggy paddle? If not, ask someone to show you the motion. Now compare that to your life. If you find yourself always struggling to stay afloat, and constantly expending a lot of energy just to keep your head above the water, you will end up not only exhausted, but also unfulfilled. You are using all of your energy merely to survive. Instead, delegate some of that energy towards thriving.

Visualize your dream. This is a crucial part of dreaming and something you should absolutely take the time to do. *Allow* yourself to dream.

Close your eyes. If negativity floats to the top of your mind say, "I am in a positive space. I will not allow you to take up my thoughts. Positive thoughts only, please. I am trying to put a dream in motion."

What do you see? Angelo might see a line of people waiting at the door. Or he might see himself at a table in a lawyer's office closing on his next property. Keisha might see a warehouse with jars of pickles stacked from here to eternity, with orders pumping out on a machine. Tracy might see herself on a yacht hitting send on an email as she sets her laptop down and goes back to sipping on her lemonade. Venus absolutely saw herself smiling in a spotlight winning not one, not two, but *seven* Grand Slam titles.

I see you reading this book, holding your head high and allowing yourself the freedom to dream.

I would love to hear what you envision. Don't leave me out of the journey. I want to hear about your takeover! Let's claim it together. **Here is why *actually* doing this is important: if you cannot see it, can you really achieve it?**

Picture in your mind everything you want your life to be and then ensure every action you take moves you towards that vision.

See it in your mind and then take the next step. You've heard it said: Don't look at the whole mountain. This is because if people really took in the height and the breadth of what they are about to scale, no one would have ever made it to the top of one. You only have to think about taking the next step. That's your only assignment. *Then take the next step.*

I have a confession to make: I take rejection really hard. That is because in the past, I have taken rejection personally. But here is a difficult lesson I learned about why you shouldn't:

When someone tells you no, they are doing you a favor.

Okay, okay, I know you are saying something like, this is just something you told yourself to make you feel better about being rejected, *but no*, this is real. And I learned it the hard way, so hear me out. When you finally open up and share your vision with someone, don't you want them to be as excited as you are? Don't you want them to scream a resounding, "YES! I am in! Where have you been all my life!?"

This was an incredibly difficult lesson for me to learn—to be grateful for all of the nos and all of the roadblocks. It takes a little brain-bending to get on this level, but it is true. If you ask someone for help and they say no, be grateful that they did. *They were not meant to be a part of your story.*

If you ask someone for help and they say no, be grateful that they did. *They were not meant to be a part of your story.*

Maybe they knew something you did not. Maybe they knew they were not right for you, even before you knew it. Or maybe they're just a jerk. In any of these scenarios, aren't you glad they bailed out? Don't be hurt or offended. Don't waste a minute of time trying to figure out why. Cross them off the list and *keep it moving*.

You don't have to have money or be well-connected to make your dreams become a reality. But you do have to *make* money and you do have to *get* connected. ***And you can.***

You may have heard the name Quinta Brunson. She is the creator of the ABC series, *Abbott Elementary*, a hit show with multiple awards. Quinta Brunson was no different from you and me. She was not rich. She was not connected to Hollywood inner circles. She had a dream. I kid you not, she started a video series on Instagram that went viral. That was where she built her first fan base—on a *free* platform that you and I *also* have access to.

It was lucky that the sketches went viral, but she also put in the work to make that happen. She did not go from Instagram to ABC. She worked to take the next step, then the next. All along the way she was connecting to people and telling them about her big dream. She was building every piece she needed for the day the opportunity would present itself. Many people describe *Abbott Elementary* as an overnight success because many people only saw the tip of the iceberg. Quinta's consistent effort and her vision paid off.

She took care of her dream, and her dream took care of her.

There are hundreds of thousands of these stories. Jim Carrey wrote himself a $10,000,000 check. Oprah Winfrey manifested her role in *The Color Purple*, later telling a talk show host that the way you think creates your reality. In 2014, Megan Thee Stallion posted on social media, "I need a team [because this rap career is about to] take off for me." She declared that *years before* her career took off. Lady Gaga repeated an affirmation of success to herself every single day until the success was real. I could give you pages of examples about the power of having a mindset that practices the art of sticktoitiveness.

My point is that we see people like Lady Gaga and Beyoncé and we say, "Wow, these people are powerhouses, completely unlike anything we see in this world!" When the truth is, that not very long ago, they would have been living right next door to us. Walking to the mailbox just like us. Carrying their trash to the curb. Just like us.

They are not superhuman. They are super entrepreneurs. The only difference is they did it. They put their dream in motion. There is no reason why you cannot do it too. *You absolutely can.* Look up some of the stories of people you admire that are in your field and read about how they made it happen. Authors, restaurateurs, chefs, motivational speakers, artists, and entrepreneurs. We all start somewhere.

And then there is me…

I grew up in Louisville, Kentucky. More specifically, Old Louisville, which is basically downtown. My family was not rich or well connected, but we were hard working. And we were dreamers. My entire family is filled with people who see a problem and want to work to address that problem.

As a child, however, I lacked motivation. My dreams were discouraged by my teachers. I barely skated by in school and always felt everything I learned in the classroom was a waste of time. Something I'd never use again. Somehow, I managed to graduate from high school. I chose the college I went to based on how many friends I had who were also attending there. I failed out my freshman year. For years, I never told anyone this or talked about it. But today it is important for me to use this experience to help others.

You can be inspired to start a new dream, even after failure. Failure is not an end. Failure is a portal.

It transports you to a hill (or maybe a valley) with a view you would have never had if it were not for that failure.

You need that failure. It will make you better. If nothing else, it will damn sure remind you of where you never want to be again.

Failure is not
an end. Failure
is a portal.

Don't buy into the myth that failure defines who you are. *Failure is just a lesson.* It's a shift in perspective.

Don't buy into the myth that there is a timeline to do anything. There are so many ways to get where you are going, and it is *never* too late to start again.

What turned it around for me? Learning that I was pregnant with my daughter at the age of twenty. I was a single mother (or would be soon) with no focus and no motivation. *Until* I became a mother.

Instantly, my purpose kicked in: *my daughter.* Or more specifically, my life with another mouth to feed and me with no direction, no career or education, and no money. I realized that I needed to do more with my life for her, even if I wouldn't do it for myself. If I ever had plans to show her how to take care of herself, I had to take care of me.

I returned to college and took advantage of every opportunity, even though I had no idea where I would end up or how I would get there. I just started doing *something.* I involved myself in as many college clubs and activities as I could without having any idea of what opportunities they could bring into my life. Most importantly, I went to a college that facilitated dreaming. This time I did not pick a school based on where my friends were spending their weekends partying. This time I selected Bennett College, an HBCU. Or maybe Bennett College selected me. Either way, I was lovingly placed in the right environment at the right time. Bennett College gave me the nurturing education I desperately needed. Bennett College gave me the foundation to launch my dreams.

After college, I started a career as a state employed social worker, which was rewarding—for a while. Eventually, I figured out that I could only get so far, and my time never seemed to belong to me. I did not like getting menial raises years apart, or having to ask anyone to take a day off, or sitting in a box, or having to report to places that made my stomach hurt, like court or the hospital.

My state job offered a free program that allowed me to further my education. I took as many classes as I could that the state would pay for. And after I fulfilled all the obligations associated with that employment benefit, I left that job and opened my own therapy company. That was scary, but I made a leap. I heard my grandmother's voice in my head telling me that I would be old one day and would need a pension. "There's work at the post office," She would say only half-way joking. I did not have my safe pension anymore, but you know what I did have? Time and energy. Time and energy that allowed me to start writing children's books based on my work as a therapist. *I had found my passion.*

Now my purpose is to help others live the life of their dreams—all the while, having the ability to control my own time and build true generational wealth for my family.

My passion is building dreams, building businesses, and writing stories for others that will be a beacon of hope. Stories that remind you that wherever you started, or wherever you are, is not where you have to stay.

I have achieved *gigantic* dreams. Owning two homes. Owning my own business. Owning my own commercial building. Employing dozens of people. Helping thousands more move towards better mental health and the life of their dreams. *I fund my own retirement account.* I pay for my own health insurance. I have published multiple award-winning and best-selling books. And when I realized my community was a book desert, I founded a large, now nationally recognized book festival to call attention to literacy issues affecting my city and state and a nonprofit that pays kids to read. And if you had asked me in my twenties if I would have done any of this, I would not have been able to predict the course I am on now. This is the locomotive effect I referred to earlier. You have no idea the impact or reach you will have until you actually get the engine on the track and *get to going*!

I am now an expert in business ideation, branding, publishing, and mental health. And I am not done. My dreams have definitely been like a high-speed train, with cars that keep connecting along the journey. Remember when I mentioned Broadway at the very beginning of the book? I am working hard to produce a Broadway show called *Modern-Day K* based on one of my children's book series, *Kayla: A Modern-Day Princess*. It is by far the biggest dream I have ever had. And the most intimidating. But there is that well-known saying you have probably heard: *If your dreams don't scare you, they're not big enough.*

I have had lots of big dreams, which included writing this book. And they were always scary … until they were done. I guess from that perspective, this one is no different. But this dream is perhaps the one most out of my control because of the time, resources, and connections it takes to produce a show on Broadway.

Among other things, I need fifteen million dollars to get to Broadway. But it's entirely possible. Shows get to Broadway every day. It's all out there. There are multiple people who will contribute fifteen million dollars, in whole or part, without blinking an eye.

I just have to go get it.

Knowing that it is out there is all I need to get going. Every day I take a step towards my dreams. I am sharing these steps with you to give you some idea of what you can also do to move towards your dreams.

I look up people who are producing shows similar to mine and add them to a spreadsheet.
I read articles about those people and take notes on their interests.

I follow them on social media and read what they post about.

I try to figure out why they are producing whatever show they are involved with now.

I DM and email people to connect.

I ask to meet people in person.

I ask if they will read my show synopsis.

I joined a Facebook group filled with other creators like me.

I study their stories and their journeys.

I write more about what it is I envision this show to be.

I met with a few Broadway producers as consultants. Some charged me. Some didn't.

I attended an annual conference called BroadwayCon in New York and attended sessions about how people make Broadway shows happen.

I also had a lot of fun at BroadwayCon, which further confirmed I am on the right path.

I joined a group of Broadway producers.

I go to as many Broadway shows as I can to study what this magic looks like from as many angles as I can.

I checked out books on Broadway from the library—some about different Broadway shows, and some about the lives of famous Broadway people like Stephen Sondheim.

I bought a book I was really interested in (instead of checking it out at the library) called *The Business of Broadway* because I loved it so much I wished I could mark it up! My mind was flooded with notes I wanted to better study. I did not want to forget all the advice given in that book about what it takes to get to Broadway from someone who researched *this exact topic.*

When I walk, I listen to Broadway soundtracks to analyze how the story is told through music. I also think about what parts of the music and the lyrics really move me so I can have a better idea of what I hope to see (or hear) in the music in my show.

I visualize why I want to do this, what it would look like, and who it would help.

I keep a journal and document it *all.*

Don't be overwhelmed by this list. I didn't do this in a day. I did all of these things over the last three years. Many of these things can be done on a break from work or in the fifteen minutes before you go to bed. And this is just a partial list of some of the things I have done. *I'm not finished.*

This dream is not easy or quick, but it is something I'm dedicated to. It absolutely can happen. I hang on to that. **This dream can happen.** And every day I do *something* to take a step towards that dream.

My daughter, who is also from Louisville, Kentucky, achieved a gigantic dream and made it as a successful Broadway actress. Keisha's mother was wrong. Broadway actress Kayla Pecchioni (still can't believe I can place those words before my baby girl's name) is on Broadway and has been in successful Tony Award-winning shows like *Paradise Square, Some Like It Hot*, and *The Great Gatsby*. Some people might think that's a connection, but not really. I mean … it doesn't hurt. But even as an actress in their shows, she's a long way from having pull with any producers.

But I bring her up now to tell this touching story, which I hope you will hold on to. My beautiful daughter Kayla, protector of my heart and original source of my inspiration, and who is *not* a hater even a little bit, said to me one day, "Mama, I hope you will not be at the end of your life and be upset if this Broadway thing doesn't work out." Kayla has seen how hard I work on every dream I go after. She has a front row seat.

Her words were warm, kind and full of care for my spirit. I simply told her, "I won't, baby. I don't want you to worry about that. I will only be at the end of my life and upset if I never try."

Sometimes the journey is more the goal than the goal itself. Take the journey.

Get it out of your head that this kind of freedom only happens to special people who feel larger than life, like Oprah and Lady Gaga.

This kind of freedom only happens to the *bold*.

Sometimes the journey is more the goal than the goal itself. Take the journey.

Be **BOLD** and join a group of people with a positive mindset.

Be **BOLD** and cut the people from your life who crush your spirit.

Be **BOLD** and write your dream down on paper. *Now it's real.*

Visualize your dream (*and you in it*). This is how to dream while you are awake.

Daydreams are not a waste of time.

Give *yourself* the first fifteen minutes of every day so you can get clear on where your energy will go each day.

Decide on one thing that you can and will accomplish today.

Make an action plan. (What 5-10 steps do you need to take next?)

Set goals with a timeline.

Schedule dates with your dream on your calendar. (Write it in like you would a doctor appointment!)

Reevaluate the goals and timeline often to ensure you are advancing.

Do not get distracted by drama in the lives of others or drama people bring to you.

Practice inhaling daily affirmations.

Stay open to things looking different than you planned. (Are you in motion? *That's* what matters.)

Just focus on what *one* thing needs to be done next.

Take at least one step a day, no matter how small. This alone adds up to 365 actions in one year towards your dream.

Never stop.

Make a way.
And a way will be made for you.

Hang on to nuggets like this. Write them down and refer back to them often when you need encouragement.

Millions and millions and millions of people have achieved their dreams. Why *not* you?

What is your dream saying to you now? Write it here:

_____

_____

_____

_____

_____

_____

_____

_____

_____

_____

Seven
Ways to Fuel Your Dream

"Don't expect it to be easy. It will not be.
But it will be worth it."

~ Me

The number one question I get, by far, is, "How do you do it?" For years, I could not put the formula into words. I could only give the answer, and the answer is, "I made a way."

Turns out the formula was not really complicated at all.

Here's the big secret.

The formula is One Step + The Next Step x The Power of Positivity = Way Made

Let's go back for a moment to my time as a state employee. I cannot count the number of meetings I sat in where I would ask a question that started with "how?"

It always went like this:

Me: "How can we get X done?"
Them: "We can't get X done because (insert a hundred reasons why we cannot do something here)."
Me: "I did not ask *why* we can't get X done. I asked *how*."

Them: "But we can't do it because no one has ever done that before."

Me: "Don't give me a list of why we *can't*. Give me a list of how we *can*."

This is called the **Make a Way Mindset**.

Don't tell me that a man can walk on the moon and then tell me we can't order lunch for a meeting with the Governor. Don't tell me that I don't have a deal with a publishing house, so I cannot publish a book.

Don't tell me that a kid from Louisville, Kentucky, who was raised with no money and no connections, does not have every single thing inside of her she needs to make it happen!

Don't tell me *no*. Tell me *how*.

It takes a positive mindset to push past the tidal wave of garbage your dream will need to withstand. The sad truth is, we are trained to list all the ways that something will *not* work before we ever get to the point of thinking about how something might work. Some of us never get to that point. We are stuck looking at the mountain and thinking, "Why even try?"

You can completely unlearn this the exact same way you learned it: through repetition. *Practice*. Yes, I'm talking about *practice*.

Here is how you make practice work for you:

Don't tell me no.
Tell me how.

Go to the library.

It is completely free, and the librarians really want to help you. They are there, waiting for you to walk through the door. Start by checking out a book on a subject related to your dream and actually reading it. Treat it like a class you don't have to pay for. Get a notebook and take notes of all the things you learn from that book.

Take the pressure off. Don't feel you have to read the whole book. Just take it a chapter at a time. If the library does not have a book on your dream subject, don't be afraid to ask. Sometimes they will order the book, or transfer it to your branch so it is easier for you to pick it up. This is a great place to start.

Tell the librarians what you are working on. They might not only point you to books. They also have a lot of insight into programs and community connections too!

Put a limit on social media.

Social media has definitely helped me stay abreast of what's happening on Broadway. I live in Kentucky. That's like a thousand miles away from the "Great White Way." Social media is important to me, but I have to keep it in check.

If you're anything like I was before I decided to prune hours a day off the time I give social media, you're going to recognize yourself in this unfortunate tale about a rabbit hole. How many times have we seen an interesting story on social media and read that story? That may have been an appropriate use of five minutes, but it doesn't end there, does it? No, now I have got to go look at the profile of the person who posted the story.

I need to peruse their entire profile and see if they were a proponent of the story or making a mockery of it. Depending on how that shakes out, I might not want to be their friend anymore, and—wait a minute—when did they get engaged? When did they get divorced in order to get engaged and can I tell from these photos who got custody of the kids and the house? They went to the zoo as a group without me and my kids? When did that happen, and how do they know so-and-so, who was also there at the zoo? Now I am six pages away from the original article on so-and-so's profile and I don't even know them. But I want this recipe they posted for a dinner party I also was not invited to! Why would I have been? I don't know them, remember?

See where I am going with this. Oh, you thought it was just you? No, it is all of us. And just another way things have been designed to keep us busy.

Some social media companies employ psychologists to figure out how to keep us on their platform as long as possible while engaging in maximum content. You got an alert on your phone to read one five-minute article and two hours later, not only have you forgotten that initial article, but to top it all off, you feel really bad.

What was that you were saying about having no time to pursue your dream? I couldn't hear you over that Beyoncé reel.

Download an app that limits the time you can spend on apps and get your life—which cannot be found on an app—back.

Look around you. The evidence that dreams come true is literally everywhere: restaurants, trampoline parks—even a tire store. Someone saw a need and made it their dream to address it.

Make a map.

Be sure you know where you are going and how to get there. It is incredibly difficult to achieve a goal until you can get clear on what it is. The power of the dream is not really in the dreaming, it's in the doing. A map puts the daydream in motion. It also helps you clarify your steps, allowing you to turn down opportunities that don't align with your purpose and could knock you off the right path.

Out of the blue I was offered a job as a professor in a graduate counseling program at a local university. I was so honored to be considered that I almost said yes immediately. I went back to my map. and even though the offer was flattering, it would not help me get where I needed to go. If you don't know your path, how will you know when you are veering away from your destination? Being a teacher is a great deal of work, and ultimately, I did not have the time I needed to dedicate to that role and still be able to accomplish my own dreams (like finishing this book).

Become the expert in your area.

Picking up a book at the library is the first step. Next step: bookstores! One of my absolute favorite things to do is visit my local bookstore. Make it a date. Take the kids. There is a way to fit this into your life.

I like books about Broadway. A lot of these are very expensive. They are big, like almanacs, and have a lot of colorful pictures. While I have a few, I cannot afford them all. So, I get a cup of coffee, grab a book I want to read, and plop down in the bookstore and read the book I am interested in right there. And it's all legal. There is nothing I love more than free education.

I was given another gem by Broadway producer Ron Simons, who agreed to meet with me to hear about my Broadway show dream. I can't explain to you how honored I was to meet with Ron. Black producers on Broadway are underrepresented in much the same way Black authors are underrepresented in the world of literature. Over the course of his career, he won four Tony awards and produced or contributed to shows like *Thoughts of A Colored Man* (which I saw on Broadway three times) and *Ain't Too Proud: The Life and Times of the Temptations*. His mission was to bring Black stories to Broadway and to continue offering a pathway to tell stories about underrepresented communities.

Ron also encouraged me to become an expert. He said that I did not have to be an expert about Broadway. I only had to be an expert about my show. What a relief. Another great piece of advice he gave me was to immerse myself in the Broadway world as much as possible. This gives you a chance to talk about your expertise.

Don't be afraid to reach out to people. Most people really do want to help. Often, they just receive more requests than they can filter through. It was Ron who told me he had 100,000 unopened emails in his inbox. He said he had no choice but to delete them all and start over. Guess when I reached out to him? Right after he deleted those messages. You never know why someone responds or what is going on in their life. I just got lucky and reached out to him right after he wiped his email slate clean.

Sadly, as I was writing this book, I learned that Ron Simons passed away. Thank you, Ron, for spending time with me. You are forever a part of my journey. Tony-nominated producer Lamar Richardson wrote, "A huge tree has fallen in the Black Broadway community. Ron walked so that many of us could run in this industry."

Document the journey.

Much like Ron had a dream of helping people tell their story on Broadway, I have a dream of telling a story on Broadway, but I also dream of helping people write their own stories and turn them into book form. So, what am I doing while I am writing this book? Writing down every step along the way. I am documenting how I did it so I can help someone else. *This* dream is fueling the *next* dream.

Somewhere there is someone who is trying to do exactly what you are right now. Your story is important and can help others. What are you learning about the industry you aspire to be a part of? *More importantly, what are you learning about you?* Write down all of the things you are learning and all of the epiphanies and the new ideas you have, or you will most likely lose this wisdom.

The best part? This is also how you become an expert. You can turn this whole journey into a book or a documentary or a class that will inspire others. Dreams come true in all sorts of ways. Don't leave what you are learning on the table. Pack it up and carry it with you.

Another benefit of this habit is that you will be able to reflect on your journey with a broader rearview mirror. The gift of introspection, insight, and hindsight is priceless.

Dreams build on one another. You don't have to do it all today. I never planned to be or do all the things I am and do today. Everything just came together like a rich and hearty stew you cannot rush.

The best dreams are rooted in a desire to help other people. My dream was not to become a social worker. Although that is an absolutely beautiful dream, it just wasn't mine. Without that experience, however, I would not have gained the introspection and insight that I needed to become a lawyer. Becoming a lawyer led to me wanting to be a therapist, which led to me wanting to be an author, which led to me being here, now, talking to you. Dreams open doors.

Your dream will be the guidepost someone else uses when they are just getting started on their own path to the freedom that only dreams can bring. Be a blessing to others. The most successful dreams allow the dreamer to be a gift to others. How does your dream help you help others in the way that Ron was able to help me?

Celebrate.

Dreams are not easy. Document your journey and celebrate it all. You are doing something that millions of people a day, maybe billions of people a day, all over the world, tell themselves they cannot do. *And you are no longer one of them.*

That is something to celebrate.

At the beginning of the year, I made a list of all the things I wanted to achieve this year. Some were huge, like writing this book, but some were smaller, like connecting with a person. All in all, there were about twenty items on the list. Around July I started feeling like a slug who had not done much, including not being done with this book. I pulled my handwritten list out of all the things I hoped to accomplish this year and guess what? I had done about half of them. I was right where I needed to be at the halfway point of the year.

That is something to celebrate.

Without that list, however, I would have still been feeling like not much had changed. I had a renewed sense of energy and I knew that if I could get those things done from January to July, I was well on my way to completing the rest by December.

Mark your milestones in the same way we celebrate birthdays or the New Year. Milestones are important. Without them, things can become a blurry mess. Milestones are also great for reflecting on what you have learned through hindsight. You never want to throw away that opportunity to stop, reflect, proceed. Don't live in hindsight, but definitely reflect on the journey.

Nelson Mandela said, "*Remember to celebrate milestones as you prepare for the road ahead.*" Do you know this man's story? It's worth studying. If Nelson Mandela can learn to celebrate milestones, you most certainly can add this to your routine, too. Even the small wins need to be acknowledged. Fuel your dream with concrete steps, action, milestones, reflection, *and* celebration. All are very important parts of the journey you are on.

Ways to fuel your dream when you have no money and no connections

Go to the library.
Read books.
Keep a notebook.
Take a free online course.
Attend a workshop.
Network.
Go to events.
Be present.
Pay attention.
Smile and behave *warmly*.
Keep your body posture open.
Ask questions.
Keep track of the answers.
Become the expert in your area.
Visit your dream (a coffee shop, a Broadway show, a university).
Put a limit on social media.
Make a map of your dream.

Document the journey.

Learn something about your dream every week (if not every day).

Research others who are doing what you want to do.

Reach out to those people and ask them a question about how they did it.

Be prepared to offer them something—even as small as a cup of coffee.

Be mindful about dreams. They are literally everywhere.

Use the dreams you see to remind you that they happen every day.

Visualize your dream *with you in it.*

Find a mentor.

Join a group of like-minded people.

Cut from your life (or severely limit) the people who kill your dreams.

Help someone else.

Ways to fuel your dream when you have no time

I am not going to sugarcoat this. If you bought this book, you are ready to get serious.

You have to make the time.

We all have it. We all love to say we don't.

Remember I said dreams aren't easy? Here's your first challenge: *What are you willing to give up to make your dreams a priority?*

If you are just going to sit there and say you don't have the time, then you are missing the point. The book is called *How To Dream,* and if you want this to work, you need to give your dreams the time and attention they deserve.

Now let's carve it out. Do you work out? Great. Download a free podcast about inspiration or about the area you want to be in and start listening to it while you exercise. Do you commute to work? This tip works there too.

Do you have to sit in a carpool lane? Perfect. Roll down the window. Let the sun shine on your face. Turn your phone on silent and start working on your map.

How are you spending your breaks? It is perfectly fine to tell the people you usually eat with that you have a call to make or an email you need to write or read.

What does your time on social media look like? You really should track it. You might be shocked to find out. Replace the time you spend surfing social media with something more meaningful, like taking a class or meeting with a supportive group to discuss your idea.

Bottom line: if you have no money and no connections, then time is all you've got. Spend your minutes like you're spending hundred-dollar bills. And give your dreams the home they deserve.

If you have no
money and no
connections,
then time is all
you've got. Spend
your minutes like
you're spending
hundred-dollar
bills.

Write these words:

I do not expect it to be easy. It will not be. But it will be worth it. It will be worth it. It will be worth it.

_____

_____

_____

_____

_____

_____

_____

List three blocks of time in your day you can give to your dreams.

_____

_____

_____

_____

_____

_____

_____

Dream Affirmations
Eight

"What you get by achieving your goals is not as important as what you become by achieving your goals."

~Johann Wolfgang von Goethe

It happened again. *To me.* You know, the person writing this book? The therapist? The professional dreamer? Yes, me. Something walked into my mind and took a seat. I didn't open the door. I didn't even hear the knock. I was minding my own business. And bam! There it was.

I don't know if it was fear or doubt or negativity. Hell, it was probably all three. All I know is it said from the *inside* of my mind *to* my mind, "You are stupid." And it happened before I could stop it.

In the past, I would have retreated to my bed for the remainder of the day. It almost took me down, but I grabbed it. I grabbed the words and talked back to them. I said, "Who the heck are you and why do you keep showing up here just to say this? I am *not* stupid. It's not true. You know it is not true. And *I* know it is not true."

I know this is not true because I know the mountains I have already conquered. Every single one made me stronger, tougher, smarter, and more unshakeable. *But even I* still have that voice that loves to tell me I haven't done anything special at all. That everything I've managed to achieve was all luck. A fluke. And it will never happen again.

Who do these words belong to? Lucky for me in my case, they are not the words of my parents. But in your case, they might be. They could be a grandparent, an ex, a competitor, a third-grade teacher, or the devil himself. Wherever they came from, I know the only thing that matters:

These words are not true.

Yet, here they are. Visiting me without permission on a sunny Sunday afternoon. In my own damn house.

You know how you usher this voice out of your head? With a broom, a dustpan, and lots of powerful, positive affirmations.

Are you gonna move full speed ahead? Then you're gonna need to toughen up. Your muscles need weights. Your brain needs words.

Do you remember earlier in the book when I mentioned "inhaling" positive affirmations? This is a term I use a lot in therapy, and there's a good reason why this is so powerful. Inhaling words means doing something more than what we usually do with words.

Have you ever had an argument where the other person swears you never told them something, even though you know you did? We've all been there. We hear words, but we don't always take them—we don't let them live in our brain. It happens so often because we cannot possibly hold on to all the pieces of information we get in a day. Many of the words we "hear" come into our ears, but bounce right off our brain and back out to where they came from.

Ever had a great day where a thousand things went right, but for some reason you can only focus on the one thing that went left? Words work in the same way.

If our minds were better trained to hold on to those thousand positive things, we would be in much better shape to dismiss the one jerk we had an unfortunate encounter with. Instead, we lay our head on our pillow at night, completely unable to stay grateful for the thousand blessings, then fall asleep cursing that single negative event.

Inhaling affirmations is more than saying the words. It's more than hearing the words. It's more than reading the words on a sticky note you hung above your bed.

Inhaling affirmations means that you breathe the words in and let them travel throughout your body. You invite the words to live in your mind. You let the words take root. You welcome them and give them room to grow. This means as the new words set up shop and take hold, the old words get evicted. But it takes time for the old words to get the eviction notice.

Sometimes words just bounce off the back of our forehead, but we are not truly taking them in as a part of who we are, or carrying them with us on our journey. You need these words with you on the trip. Then that one bad thing or one not-so-nice person can't touch your spirit.

One of the most important dream affirmations I want you to hold on to is that *you have the right to dream.*

Dreaming is a part of our birthright.
Dreaming is how we find out who we are and why we were meant to be here.
Dreaming is what allows your destiny to unfold.
Dreaming is how we make sure that our lives remain our lives to live.
Your life does not belong to someone else. **Your life belongs to you.**

Dreaming is freedom of the mind, heart, and soul.

It is the fuel you need to live your life to the fullest.

All kids play and dream … How did we lose it?
More specifically, how did you lose it? Your precious ability to dream?
Maybe someone made fun of your dreams.
Or someone told you that you were silly for dreaming.
Someone told you dreams were a waste of time.
Maybe someone told you that you were stupid.
Maybe you did not have role models who dreamed.

Dreaming is freedom of the mind, heart, and soul.

Or maybe you did not have adults in your life who *talked* about dreams, so it was never modeled for you. Perhaps somewhere along the way, dreams became painful for them, and that pain and fear of dreaming was transferred to you. Maybe, in your family, dreams felt out of reach.

During the times in your life when you felt hopeless, dreams seemed impossible. It took every ounce of energy you had just to come back from that time period, and you had no energy to dedicate to anything but your survival.

You might have also been taught that dreams are so risky that you will always be disappointed. Maybe you got the message that dreams can be painful. Why even try?

Part of your journey should be about the journey itself. How can you lose when you are working on you? Keep working on the inside, so you are ready for whatever is on the outside.

Believing you can is so important that I'm dedicating an entire chapter to the power of affirmations.

Believe you *can* and you will be absolutely right.
Believe you *can't* and you will also be just as right.
Which right do you want to be?

How to get the most out of affirmations

Positive affirmations are mind shifts. They are very powerful and very easy to use. Get into the habit of using affirmations every day. You can get into the habit of anything. If you can brush your teeth every day, you can say your affirmations every day.

Repeat them regularly. Some of y'all won't know what I'm talking about, but there used to be these things called cassette tapes. We could record what we wanted on the cassette tape and listen to it over and over again. Mostly, we recorded songs off the radio. Sometimes we recorded people—an interview for school or a grandparent retelling a story we did not want to forget. Your brain is a lot like that cassette tape. We all have stories we tell ourselves, and many of them are on autoplay. Affirmations help you write over the negative messages on the tape that is your mind. If you inhale the affirmations enough, you might not even remember that there was anything else on that old tape.

Choose authentic affirmations. I will give you several here, but you need to use the ones that fit your journey and your needs. Like journeys, everyone's affirmations will be different.

Use affirmations in the present tense. We are not praying over the past. We are claiming what we have in this moment and what we will have in the future. If you are struggling with this, you can start your affirmations with *I can*, *I will*, *I have*, or *I am*.

Positive affirmations are how you begin to write your own story. That voice I had in my head—the one that told me that I was stupid—that came from somewhere. I clung to that word or that feeling and, even now, when I face a challenge, sometimes that word comes back up. The more I allow myself to hear the new voice in my head that *I am that girl*, the less I hear the old tape. Regular affirmations actually work in the same way as someone recording over the current message on a cassette tape. You will never be able to hear what was on the old tape again once the new recording is in place.

Believe they work. Don't just take my word for it. Do some research on the subject. Positive affirmations are backed up by science! If you don't believe in the power of affirmations and your ability to create the life you want, you will continue to sabotage yourself. Then your experiences in life will be disappointing every time.

Give them time to grow. In therapy, I often write affirmations with my clients and encourage them to carry them with them, or put them on the mirror where they brush their teeth, or hang them above their bed so they are the first thing and the last thing they see each day. How often do you think people come back a week later with their jaws tight and tell me, "Your affirmations don't work!" We did not get these negative thoughts and words in our head in a week. It will take more than a week to reverse it. Don't give up on this practice. Make it a part of your lifestyle as much as any other routine in your life.

Practice the art of gratitude. By focusing on all that you have to be grateful for, you can stop the negative bashing, the self-sabotage, and the pain that somehow keeps finding you—even when, *especially when*, it feels there is absolutely nothing at all to be grateful for. Make gratitude a part of your affirmation practice and watch as more opportunities to show gratitude emerge.

Here are some of my favorite affirmations about dreams that I have accumulated over the years.

Dream Affirmations

I have the right to dream.
My dreams are not a waste of my time.
My dream belongs to me.
I don't need anyone to approve my dream.
If I am given the dream, I will be given a way to make it happen.
My dreams are the reason why I am here.
Dreams require BIG faith.
Dreams take work.
Dreams take time.

Every day I will do something to move me closer to my dream.

I am worthy of my dreams.

Dreams are meant for everyone.

Dreams come true every day.

If someone says no, that was not the person for you.

Dream big and then dream even bigger.

I will notice the little moments of magic today.

I do not easily break. Those things designed to break me become my fuel.

I am consciously creating the person I am becoming.

When I nurture the inside, the outside will flourish.

My energy is a precious resource and I will protect it like I protect the gas in my tank.

I will no longer underestimate my own magic.

I am open to new possibilities.

I am letting go of expectations.

I welcome what is coming.

I am not afraid to try something new.

My dreams are on my heart for a reason. (The 8 year-old me is counting on me.)

Steps are rewarded.

Taking action is rewarded.

Motion is rewarded.

Effort pays off.

Here are a few more affirmations specifically designed to help you stay focused on making your dreams come true:

I am dedicated to going after my dream.
I am worthy of success and freedom.
Every day I take a step closer to my goals.
I am resilient, determined, and unstoppable.
I believe in my vision.
I will not apologize for wanting more.
I will not apologize for having ambition.
I attract opportunities that align with my goals.
Everything I want is on its way to me.
I make room in my life for success.
I don't see problems, I see pathways.
I embrace challenges because they lead to growth and improvement.
My hard work and dedication are paying off.
When I follow my heart, I am free.

Feel free to use some or all of these. Be sure to create your own. Hold on to them like you hold on to the rail on a roller coaster. They will not only help you land safely, they will keep you from getting as bruised up as you would without them.

Put them on sticky notes and place these reminders everywhere. Put them in the notes app on your phone. Write them down in your journal. Write them in a letter

When I follow
my heart,
I am free.

to yourself and mail it. I have some on an index card in my wallet. They seem to pop up whenever I need them the most—like paying a bill I did not expect or when I'm berating myself because I can't find my car keys.

Repeat your affirmations every day. Don't lose sight of them, ever. Repeating your individual set of affirmations daily can help reinforce your commitment, buoy you, and keep you pushing through. Your mind believes what you tell it.

Write three affirmations that you need to hear the most here:

_____

_____

_____

_____

_____

_____

_____

_____

_____

_____

Now write them on an index card and carry them with you.

Nine
Put Your Dream in Motion

*"You know I used to beat that block,
now I be's the block."*

~Jay Z

Let's chart what ten years looks like.

No dream or no action on a dream

(This equals _zero steps_ toward the life you want and deserve.)

You at 30	**You at 40**
No house	No house
No vacation to the beach	No vacation to the beach
Beaten down/ tired/ depressed	Even more beaten down/tired/depressed
No retirement savings	No retirement savings
No generational wealth to pass down	No generational wealth to pass down
Feelings of being unfulfilled	Feeling even more unfulfilled
No hope	No hope

One step a day towards a dream

(This equals _three thousand six hundred and fifty-two steps_ toward the life you want and deserve.)

You at 30	You at 40
No house	Homeowner
No vacation to the beach	Vacation
Beaten down/ tired/ depressed	Lifted/ engaged/ excited
No retirement savings	Working on retirement savings
No generational wealth to pass down	A plan for wealth coming in or on the way
Feelings of being unfulfilled	Feeling rewarded for effort
No hope	Hope in spades

We want everything overnight or next week. Life does not work like that. In this context, _life is long_. You have the time. Even if you do not actually achieve the "big" dream … say getting a show to Broadway, you still win. It's that whole "shoot for the moon and you'll land among the stars" idea. Effort will be rewarded. Motion, in conjunction with a plan, will be rewarded.

> Time moves. There is nothing you can do to stop it, slow it down, or turn it back. The only thing you can do is move right along with it.

You can sit exactly where you are and continue being too afraid to move, but time will never be afraid to tick to the next minute. Ten years will pass whether you want it to or not. I want you to have something to show for those ten years—to be able to look back at all the milestones, good and bad, and to celebrate how far you have come.

What do the next ten years look like for you? Have you thought about that?

More importantly, have you written that down? Because here's another thing about time: when you are not documenting the journey, time gets away from you. *And it can get away from you quickly.*

You might be having lunch with a friend in a café when the friend says, "Hey whatever happened to that idea that you had to change the world?" And you answer, "Oh yeah, that's definitely been in my five-year plan." Then your friend hesitates to break the news to you that you told them this idea eight years ago. It creeps up quick!

If you don't write the dream down and move towards it, time will change. You will not.

Yes, I heard what you said. And I said that too. You're not ready. I know. I get it.

True story: Once I wanted to grow the newsletter audience for my consulting business using a lead magnet. But I could not come up with a good idea for a short two-to-three page lead magnet that would accurately reflect what I wanted to say about the work I do. Or more specifically, why anyone should work with me. So, you know what I did? I started downloading the lead magnets of other people. And of course as is the way in the world of social media, all I had to do was download a couple and then my timeline was flooded with them.

People get you to download their lead magnet so they can get your contact information. Then they start emailing you three times a day with their "special" offers. Before I knew it, my email box was a mess. Worse, another month had passed, and I hadn't read a single lead magnet.

This is what we call a distraction. Was I taking a step? Sure, but it was in the wrong direction. This wasn't really helping me, so I had to reassess and unsubscribe to a whole lot of stuff. The lead magnets never helped me because they were not *my* message. It would have served me better to just strap in and work on my own message, as opposed to thinking that I could find my message in someone else's work. But I lacked confidence in my message—I was just starting out.

You will never feel completely ready to do the thing you are about to do. Do it anyway.

You will never feel completely ready to do the thing you are about to do. Do it anyway.

The feeling of being ready never comes. Most of the time it is after you have done the thing that you look back, shrug your shoulders and say, huh, I guess I was ready after all.

Remember what I said about your sticktoitiveness power? You already have all you need. You can do this.

You know how I know you can do it? Because if you couldn't, you would have never been given the dream.

If the dream finds you, so will the way.

Seth Godin, a teacher, entrepreneur, and master marketer once said, "The only thing worse than starting something and failing ... is not starting something."

You have the idea. Take the step.

Make a plan.

Make it stick.

Do you have any idea where you will be in ten years?

Perhaps there is no rapper that better illustrates the American Dream like Shawn Corey Carter. Better known to us now as Jay-Z, he grew up in a New York City housing project and began selling drugs at the age of twelve.

It is important that you not interpret selling drugs at the age of twelve as a reflection of character, but as a reflection of circumstances. Even when he started rapping, he noticed that many rappers were still broke. Selling drugs helped him support his family after his father left. But as Jay-Z also famously sang in a song, "I'm not a businessman, I'm a business, man." He had his mind set on doing something different. Contributing to the uplifting, rather than the decline, of his community became part of the impetus he needed to find his passion. In other words, he used to beat the block, now he *is* the block. Because there were not many options, he used to have to hustle on the block. Then he made his own options, and *now he owns the whole damn block*!

Don't tell me dreams don't come true. Don't tell me effort is not rewarded. Don't tell me you still don't believe in the power of *you*. Jay-Z is me. Jay-Z is you.

Jay-Z came from the projects of New York City and became the first ever hip-hop billionaire, with well over one hundred million records sold, two dozen Grammys, a clothing line, multiple properties, and several other multi-million-dollar businesses and ventures.

Billionaire status is rare. There are less than three thousand in the entire world, but that's not my point. The point is, you can come from anything, and start anywhere, and make your dream happen. Jay-Z's life at thirty and Jay-Z's life at forty feel like two completely different lifetimes, but they are not. Ten years in this man's life made all the difference in the world. A career in entertainment is not

"I'm not a
businessman,
I'm a business,
man."

easy. In fact, it can be very cutthroat. But he never gave up. He didn't get distracted. He was confident in his own message.

Not giving up is the only way you can truly test whether or not your dream is real.

If you need a break, take a break. But do not quit dreaming. When you give up on having dreams, you give up on yourself.

Strategies to kickstart your dreaming engine

Here is my number one tip: Have fun with it! Work is work. Dreams are work, but they are also a whole lot of fun.

For nearly ten years, I only wrote books for children. I find the thinking of children to be magical. It is fun to write for children because they still believe in, well, everything. What if we never lost that? How much more creative and full of invention would we be?

Lin Manuel Miranda had to tell a hundred people that he was writing a Broadway show—full of rap—about a founding father of the United States of America. How absolutely fun! What kind of leap do you think that required before he got any kind of acknowledgement that anyone other than him saw the magic in his vision? What responses and facial expressions must he have received? Thank God he didn't listen. And today we have *Hamilton*, one of the most popular, long-running musicals of all time.

Once I met an adult whose dream as a child was to be a butterfly. Her parents did not discourage this dream. They did not tell her that her thoughts were ridiculous or to focus on something more practical. No one said, of course humans can't be butterflies, silly! Instead, her parents took her to NASA and science museums, where she learned all about the science of aeronautics. They had fun with it. She got tinkerbell wings at Disney World and they raised Monarch butterflies they called her "real" family. You know what she turned out to be? An airline pilot. Turns out she was a butterfly after all!

Sometimes our heart tells us what we want to be even before we have all the words. How will you ever know if you never breathe life into your dreams and have a little fun with the idea?

I always wanted to write. I had stories calling out to me, begging me to put them on paper. Then life happened. There was always something else going on. Something else needing my attention. Something else on fire. And I suppose I also lived in fear. I allowed those little cuts I talked about earlier to get to me. Things like, "What do you have to say that's new?" or "Why would people want to read what you have to say?" I had to dig down deep and draw on what I know from the practice of mindfulness to get the nerve to write and publish my first book.

And I did that. I published my first book at forty-four years old. I didn't buy into our societal myths that I was too old to try something new. And I knew that there would be someone somewhere who would need the words I write. My dream is not just a blessing to me. My dream is a blessing to others.

I also had to get a little cocky, though we have been told we should be anything but. I think most authors need to be a little arrogant about their work. Not arrogant towards other human beings, but arrogant about the message they have to deliver to the world.

Yeah, just like Venus, I'm gonna need you to get a little cocky about your message.

A thousand books may have been written on whatever subject is calling your name. It might be romance or fantasy or self-help … but **no book has ever been written by *you*.** And that is where your magic lies. *You have something to say.* And no one on the planet can deliver the message that you were called to deliver. That dream belongs solely to you.

This is the kind of magic that happens when we allow ourselves to focus on how to bring the dream to life, as opposed to all the reasons why becoming a butterfly is never gonna work out.

Lastly, **let go of the feeling that you need to have it all figured out**. You don't. You may be doing something that has never been done before. Or you may just be doing something where there is no handy guide available.

David E. Talbert wrote and directed *Jingle Jangle: A Christmas Journey*. This was a movie unlike anything we had ever seen before. Fantasy? Holidays? 1800s? Black people? Dreaming? And it all worked because it was *his* vision. It was his passion and his message. David wanted to create a story like this for two decades, and it all came together exactly when it was supposed to happen. For twenty years, this dream was in motion—and it paid off. *Big*. Back to our talk about not needing to have it all figured out, hold on to what David said in an interview about this dream: "There's a great freedom in having never done something before. You don't know the rules, so therefore you don't know you're breaking them."

Often, we are not aware of the rules that have been laid down for us. Other people dictate that things must be done a certain way. The reasoning? Because that's the way it's always been. But they never met *you*. Breaking rules can be a lot of fun, but you need to develop that cockiness I keep talking about because your message will be challenged and you need to be ready.

I had a dream to start the Louisville Book Festival. I had absolutely no idea what it would take. Honestly, just between you and me—had I known, I probably wouldn't have done it. (Remember what I said about not looking at the whole mountain?) I wish I could report to you that it's been all sunshine and rainbows. It has not. In fact, I was taken off guard by some of the resentment I faced for trying to do something that, in my view, had nothing but a complete upside for the city I live in.

After the third "Who do you think you are?" email was delivered to my inbox, I was sitting in my office staring at the wall. I had begun to question if this venture was worth it when someone I was mentoring at the time wandered in. I told her what happened and then said, "I don't understand it. Why would I face backlash for trying to do something good?" She replied, "Because you *are* doing something good. And good will always face pushback because evil will always try to stop good."

Good sent me a message that day. And I have not looked back since.

Still, the festival is a lot of work. I mean *a lot a lot*. I only knew it was needed and that it was something that could benefit my entire community.

What's my dream affirmation for the Louisville Book Festival?

I am planting a tree.

The festival will outlive me; there will be people from all over the world who will sit in its shade for years to come. I had no idea the lives that it would actually go on to touch— people who do live in Louisville, or in Kentucky, or even in the United States! I can't let pettiness or misunderstandings get in my way.

People are always gonna people. I ignore all that. I *only* listen to the dream. I just talk to the dream and say, "Okay, Louisville Book Festival, what's the next step?"

Just because we do not know how to make something happen does not mean that it is not possible to make something happen. **There is freedom in you trusting the journey that you are on and charting your own course.**

Your dream is not this big gigantic unattainable thing. Your dream can be achieved by breaking it down into smaller, more manageable, doable goals. Your big dream is just a series of small steps you need to take.

We've talked about a lot and I don't want to lose this point because this will absolutely be what *puts* your dream in motion and what *keeps* it in motion: just take the next step. As long as you keep doing that, your dream is in motion.

To summarize this strategy:

Have fun with it.

Explore your dream.

Don't think you have to have it all figured out.

Just take the next step. (I'm never going to stop saying this because it is in the fear between the last step and the next step that people quit.)

Learn to rest, not quit.

Believe there is room for you.

Don't be afraid to do something completely different.

Get cocky about your message and your vision. You are the expert on that!

Trust your journey, even if you face pushback. Ignore the noise.

Remember, you are planting a tree. People will sit in the shade you provide for decades.

What does your life look like in ten years?

_____

_____

_____

_____

_____

_____

_____

_____

Ten
Become Unstoppable

"Just what made that little ole' ant, think he could move that rubber tree plant. Everyone knows an ant can't move a rubber tree plant. But he's got high hopes."

~Andrea Pecchioni

Okay. My mom, Andrea, didn't really say that. But she *did* used to sing that song to me and my sisters all the time. Especially when we told her that we were afraid to do something hard or new.

She was singing about a growth mindset before I even knew what a growth mindset was. Now I preach about the importance of developing a growth mindset for a living. Thank you again, mama.

Lyricist Sammy Cahn wrote the words that were popularized by the singing voice of Frank Sinatra. Many, many others went on to sing the song, including Sammy Davis, Jr., but I digress.

Picture a little tiny ant, smaller than an inch, trying to move a big basket with a three-foot tree in it. It's not gonna happen, right? Of course it is. The ant's got high hopes! *OOPS! There goes another rubber tree ....*

What my mom was singing to us was an affirmation. It is a tune that still plays in my mind to this very day, decades later. My mom has been gone from this Earth for more than twenty years and the song still comes up in my mind whenever I feel challenged. Recently I was on the phone with one of my sisters crying about a dream that feels so big it sometimes takes my breath away. Dreams sometimes feel painful—especially big dreams. My sister started singing that song and the pain went away. It was like she sent me a hug from my mom.

I was instantly reminded that I have done big things. Even scary things. I was instantly reminded of not only where I come from, but *who* I come from.

Be careful what you feed your mind. It will become your default and it will come back to visit you over and over again.

Luckily, this song is a welcome visitor.

When you get discouraged, and you will, **remember your why**.
Why did you start this journey?
Why did you pick up this book?
Why is this dream bigger than you?
Why is this dream something you must do?
Why does this dream keep talking to you?

Life is not a merry-go-round. You are not strapped in on the only horse that was left to grab. You are an active participant in your life. You are in control of this ride. Act like it!

You already have the biggest tool you need to become unstoppable: your mind—with your newly upgraded Make A Way Mindset. Start off every day protecting your mindset and your mood. Direct your energy where you *want* it to go, not where your *reactions* take you. Your newly enhanced mind will be the warrior that fends off negativity and the guard that guides your thoughts. Put up a gate and place a soldier at the door.

Take control of your mind and monitor everything that goes in and everything that goes out. Did you know your brain will believe everything you tell it to believe? That's real power. Get control of your thoughts and your emotions. You can do this. You don't have to spiral out of control because you believe you have "the right" to. No, we do not have time for that.

I want you to work on developing a growth mindset. I wish this was a term that I came up with. It is not—Carol Dweck gets that honor. But if you learn as much as you can about how to live every day with a growth mindset, it will change your life. *Growth is motion.* Working on your mind is an important part of putting your dream in motion. There is so much out there for free on how to train your mind to live in a place of growth as opposed to a fixed mindset, but here's a mini-lesson to get you started because this is how you become *unstoppable*.

Do you remember the formula?

Growth is
motion. Working
on your mind
is an important
part of putting
your dream in
motion.

One Step + The Next Step x The Power of Positivity = Way Made

Developing a growth mindset helps you with the positivity part of the equation. And let's face it, we all struggle in this area sometimes.

There will be times when it feels like your dream is under attack. You will need to know how to process what is coming your way without it completely taking you out of the game.

A growth mindset believes:

1. You can learn *anything* with time, practice, and patience.

2. Obstacles and setbacks are not closed doors; they are further opportunities to learn.

3. That you don't give up because you face a challenge.

4. Those steps you take every day are not needless mindless tasks, but necessary for you to become the expert.

5. You are open to feedback and advice. You are coachable.

6. You can learn from, rather than be discouraged by, the success of others.

7. Failing is a necessary part of learning, a lesson along the way, not a signal to quit.

People with a growth mindset are more successful than people with a fixed mindset. They know that the minute you think you know everything, you know nothing. I remember being in high school and me and my classmates believed that once we got through college, our painful hours of learning would be over. Now I know that learning is what fuels my dreams. If I'm not learning, I'm dead.

You have done hard things already. Put your dreams in your hands only. Don't be disappointed when others don't show up for you. Don't take that as a sign that your dream is not worthy of being supported.

There are whole articles about authors who are talking about book signings they held where not a single person showed up.

A fixed mindset says: I suck. I'm so stupid. Why did I think I could write a book?

A growth mindset says: I am proud of myself. I am here. I did it. I wrote the book and held a signing. Wow. Go me!

You held the event. You showed up. *You took the leap*. You did it. *You win!* Celebrate that you got to that point.

When I first started my consulting business, I really only had one faithful member who showed up for my coaching calls regularly. Once she said to me, "I am in awe of you. I remember when it was just me and you on the call, but I watched you. I watched what you would do next, and you still held the next call, and you still sent weekly emails." *I stuck with it, and now I am not where I started … but I had to start. Ten years later, I am here with you!*

If you walk away because it does not look the way you thought it would, how will you ever know what it can be?

I saw Iyanla Vanzant in person. She talked about how she started off doing motivational speaking and would get paid $50 for the whole gig—even though her expertise and wisdom were worth so much more. But she had to *start*. Now, *thousands* of people pay more than $50 a ticket *each* to see her speak. If she quit after the first $50 gig, how would she have ever gotten to the powerhouse status she is today?

A fixed mindset gets offended and quits when someone offers you $50 to show up.

A growth mindset shows up and accepts $50 until you are selling out your own auditoriums for $50 *per* ticket.

Stop making excuses for yourself. This book has shown you that not having great parents or both parents, growing up in the projects, going through divorce, not having any money, not having a college degree, having a child alone at twenty, *none* of these things are a barrier to you moving towards the life you want.

The only barrier is your mind and the fear and negativity you let live there.

The only barrier
is your mind
and the fear and
negativity you
let live there.

If you find yourself saying, "but I don't have," change that to *what you do have*. That's a growth mindset.

I've spent the book talking about people who have reached different levels of success. We need to be reminded that it is real. It is possible, but ...

Don't measure your journey by the journey of anyone else.

It's not about becoming the best version of Jay-Z. It's about becoming the best version of *you*. Jay-Z is the best version of Jay-Z.

It's not about making a billion dollars either. *It's about being free.* Anything else that comes with it is gravy.

Believe in yourself. There may be days when your belief in you is all you have. *That's* how important it is. This goes back to your purpose, which we talked about at the beginning of the book.

When you find your purpose, days when no one shows up hurts less. You are confident. You are passionate. You are living in your purpose. The only person who needed to show up that day was you.

You are a human being filled with **limitless** *potential.* You have **can do** power that has been divinely gifted to you. But **can do** power is nothing with a **can't do** mindset. You need a growth mindset. **You need a Make A Way Mindset.**

A fixed mindset says: I am not good enough.

A growth mindset says: I am good enough, so *that* settles *that*.

Dreamers are bold. Dreamers are in motion. Dreamers are a little cocky.

Who am I to dream?

I am a child of God.
I am Andrea's daughter.
I am the keeper of the bee.
I am a hard worker.
I am a good person.
I am a blessing to others.
I am bold.
I am constantly in motion.
I am a little cocky.
And I am good enough and that settles that.

Who are you?

You are a dreamer.
And you are unstoppable.

_____

_____

_____

_____

_____

_____

_____

Who are you to dream?

_____

_____

_____

_____

_____

_____

_____

_____

Two quick things you can do to help spread the word about the power of dreams:

1. Start putting your dreams in motion immediately by downloading a free journal and reflection guide at: **makeawaymindset.com/howtodreamfreeguide**

2. Leave a review wherever you bought this book or on Goodreads. It means the world to an author and only takes a minute!

Thank you for supporting *this* dream. I want to hear from you! Write to me at **deedee@makeawaymedia.com** and share your dream journey with me.

Never stop dreaming!

~Deedee

About the Author

Image credit: Irene Bibee Vine and Branch Studio

Deedee Cummings is a professional dreamer. She is also an author of nineteen books, therapist, attorney, and mom from Louisville, Kentucky. Cummings founded Make A Way Media in 2014 after struggling to find books with characters who looked like her own children and an extreme lack of stories that reflected their life experiences. Books published by Make A Way focus on hope, diversity, social justice, and therapeutic skills for children and adults. Her work has been featured in HuffPost, Forbes,

NPR, USA Today, Essence Magazine, Psych Central, Well+Good, and The EveryGirl, among other media outlets. In 2021, she was appointed to the Kentucky Early Childhood Advisory Council by Kentucky Governor Andy Beshear acknowledging her decades long service to the children and families of Kentucky. Cummings is also the founder of The Louisville Book Festival. She was inspired to work to highlight and celebrate a culture of reading in her community after working as an in-home therapist and visiting homes of children who had no books. Cummings believes literacy is a fundamental human right. Her work highlights inspiring messages that remind us all it is never too late to begin again. She is currently working to adapt her latest children's series inspired by the life of her daughter, Kayla Pecchioni (a Broadway actress) to a Broadway musical. Cummings recently founded the Make A Way Mindset program to teach the unshakable mindset she has developed as an entrepreneur of thirty years. She lives with her husband Anthony and has three children Kayla, Anthony, and Nick.